Copyright © 2009 The Ignatian Spirituality Centre of Montreal
All rights reserved.
ISBN: 1-4392-4399-9
ISBN-13: 978-1439243992

Visit www.booksurge.com to order additional copies.

Introduction

This little book has been written for those who somehow — by God's grace — experience the desire to live a more authentic kind of Christian life. Perhaps you would like to get in touch with the divine mystery in a more personal way. Or perhaps you've heard and read of prayer with Scripture passages, would like to know more about it, but hesitate to put yourself into the hands of a spiritual director right away.

Many of our older devotional practices, it should be noted, are no longer available or feel somehow disconnected with what is going forward today. Not that there's anything wrong with them in themselves.

Maybe those devotional ways will in fact go through forms of renewal that will bring them back into currency one day. After all, concrete habits of prayer are what give real substance to daily living. The Christian faith always needs to make its way into the fabric of our ordinary experience. If not, then what we believe remains abstract, unrealized.

During recent decades the age-old practice of praying with selected texts of Holy Scripture on an everyday basis has gone through exactly that sort of renewal. It wouldn't be an exaggeration to say that it has been rediscovered, not only for priests and sisters but especially for lay people.

This is not the only method of prayer being taught today, but it is certainly the most central practice of our Western spiritual tradition of personal prayer. And those who take it up afresh today are very enthusiastic.

But do you have to experience it before you can know what it's all about? In one sense that's true. When you've done it awhile you'll receive a personal taste of what's involved—for which there can be no real substitute.

But in another way I believe the method can be set forth in plain language that will make sense to those who haven't practiced it yet. That is what I'm presenting in this book. I assume my readers will be contemporary people able to judge for themselves what may or may not suit them at present. And so I try to explain matters as clearly as I can.

After each chapter there is also a short list of practical suggestions on the topics discussed. You have a right to know what might be required of you if you decide to try this method.

Should you do so, it might be the beginning of new growth for you. Perhaps you'll be able to move forward with a fresh sense of meaning and purpose in your life. But meanwhile, these pages will let you know what is involved.

Chapter 1
Pondering in the Heart

The first image of Christian prayer, given us in the gospel itself, is Mary's own "pondering in the heart." It shows us a kind of prayer that relies on memory. When St. Luke has told the story of Jesus' birth and then how the shepherds experienced a vision, heard mysterious singing, and rushed over to the stable-cave to see the Christ child, he adds (in a different tone of voice): "But Mary kept all these things, pondering them in her heart." [Lk. 2:19]

What could these events possibly mean? How would they affect her life? She needed time to get in touch with what had taken place and to learn how she might respond to them in freedom.

That is a marvelous image of interior prayer. And just in case you missed it, St. Luke repeats the same thing after his little story of Jesus' disappearance at the age of twelve.

For three whole days, Joseph and Mary searched in the city for their missing boy only to find him at last sitting among the teachers in the Temple. He seemed a bit overwhelmed, so much so that he didn't even apologize for causing them all that anxiety. Instead he spoke mysteriously to them about his future mission ("my Father's business").

At this point Mary's heart must have felt fear. What is his destiny to be? What will happen to him? Who exactly is this child of ours? Has God put something new into his heart? (It is true or is it only a delusion?) At once Luke adds again, "His mother kept all these things in her heart." [2:51]

Here we have an image of a mother brooding over strange events that have suddenly emerged in her life. Those happenings have now turned into a "nest of eggs" that will have to be kept warm. But why is all that brooding necessary? Obviously, the eggs won't be hatched unless they are tended carefully for quite a while.

TIME IS ESSENTIAL

The point is that our human experiences need attention before they can be realized. It's a mistake to imagine that new happenings in our life are immediately clear. Some events, of course, are obvious enough. But that's because they aren't very important or because we already know how to take them. They fit into present patterns.

But important new experiences that come upon us don't usually fit into known patterns. And that's what makes them fearful and shocking at first, or at least numbing and obscure. They easily throw us off balance. And we can ask ourselves, are we taking them too seriously, exaggerating them? (Exactly how should we respond? Remember that they don't become fully real until we give some kind of response to them.)

But we simply can't grasp them all at once—we need more time. There's a lot more to them than meets the eye at first. Somehow we "know" (deeper down) that they matter to us, but we have no way of speaking clearly about them right now. They are mysterious, and perhaps they include graces that will lead to changes in our life. But who can say for sure? We could choose to brood on them awhile—maybe they'll hatch later on.

On the other hand, we could let them slip away by paying them scant attention. We could simply forget about them. Or we could choose to ignore them (shoving them out of sight) because we're afraid they might mean trouble for us. And we could easily lose the gifts they bring.

Those would be very human reactions. And of course our better responses would be more positive. For example, we could be eager for new graces from God. We might be yearning to get out of a spiritual rut. We could become courageous enough to want to grow, to change, to find new life. And so we might treasure the more mysterious experiences that come to us.

That gives us another key to interior prayer: it calls for courage because it means dealing with the real issues in our life, facing things squarely in the presence of God, where there can be no lies. (But what a relief that might be, compared with stone-walling or running away!)

To sum up, then, prayer means finding time on an ongoing basis to spend on experiences that have mattered to us. What do they mean or imply, and what values do they include? Are they from God or from our Enemy?

That last question leads to another. How are we going to respond in freedom to those events? Will we say Yes to them, or will it be No? Should we put our energies into their realization? Or should we try to prevent them from having any further effect on us? Choices will have to be made. (If we don't pray about them, of course, that in itself is a choice we've already made.

A FAITH CONTEXT

Some of these points will be handled more fully later on, but for now I want to say something about the faith setting of our outer and inner experiences. Our pondering in the heart (a form of prayer done in the divine presence) does not take place in a social vacuum, isolated from all we know about God. No, what was revealed to us by Jesus Christ has been handed down to our times by the Church, taught to us in our family and schooling (if that was our way), or learned in our later life. Our faith experiences are usually connected with what we already sense about the divine mystery from our earlier contacts.

Without a certain amount of religious knowledge, prayer would be reduced to a desperate "cry in the wilderness." That is, no doubt, a kind of prayer that matters in certain situations, and God often answers such cries of near-despair. But most prayers will not be of that sort.

Mary, the mother of Jesus, as she brooded over the new events in her life, was a devout Jewish girl in Palestine who had already come to know God in the Torah, the Psalms, Prophets and History books read out reverently in her synagogue at Nazareth. She had also learned a lot from her family.

In a rich setting of that kind she received her angelic visitor's message. It was a profound experience for her, one that would lead to many further experiences. At once she was changed by it into "the Mother of God"—a girl of about fourteen! But God had been preparing her for this moment—she was, in the words of the angel, already "full of grace." [Lk. 1:28]

In other words, none of this could have come true in her life if she hadn't been able to place those experiences of God within a circle of precious beliefs which enabled her to know—to some extent, at least—what they might mean. Only a set of beliefs handed down to her could have made that possible.

She relied on the sacred knowledge of her own people. She belonged to a community of faith. We might say that God prepared her for what was to come by placing her as a faithful member of a people who believed devoutly in their divine calling. Because members of the older generations around her were believers, they taught her as a child and nourished her youthful heart in the Hebrew Scriptures (what Christians call the Old Testament).

When the Archangel descended into her chamber, Mary was ready to receive the startling message from God that Gabriel delivered. She obtained other graces, too, which enabled her after a little time to say the words, "Let it be done to me according to your word." But it seems certain she had no clear idea what it would actually mean to her in the long run.

All her life she pondered on these and later events (like her grown Son's answer, "My mother, and my brothers and sisters, are those who hear the word of God and keep it!") [Mt. 12:50]. She pondered on these strange graces until their inner powers could be released in her and flow into her whole self, into her ways of dealing with others, into her very world.

THE GOSPEL STORIES

For us, the Christian writings have been added to the Hebrew Scriptures. What was written down, under divine inspiration, had already been carefully pondered in the hearts of many believers. Since then it has been treasured in the community of faith—for Holy Scripture has rightly been called "the book of the Church."

The exact list of writings included within its covers (the "canon," as it is named) was chosen over several centuries—tested out over long years in prayer—to be handed down to future times, that is, for our benefit. It vividly tells us the story of what Jesus said and did, and what the earliest believers made of it.

But if it is to become realized today, each one of us must hear his message in the very depths of our own being. The trouble is that too many people hear only with their ears or only in their heads. But unless the mystery of Jesus' life makes an impact on our heart, it will not seriously affect our way of living in the world. That is why pondering the words of Scripture in times of prayer is a key method for bringing reality into a Christian life.

The stories of Jesus supply the faith setting needed for us to grasp the meaning of our own religious experiences. This process may help us to make them fruitful at last. The powers of the mysterious actions of God need to be found, sifted and answered by us in freedom. But that will take time. To pray each day with Scripture passages has long been the way for individual believers in Jesus to "take time" for that to come about. That's what is meant by pondering in the heart.

Practical Suggestions

1. The amount of time needed is at least thirty minutes and not longer than an hour. Experience shows that the length of time must be limited if the practice is to be done faithfully each day over the long haul. But fifteen or twenty minutes are not enough: at least half an hour is required in order to "get there" and allow some exchange to take place (a certain experience of communion with, or getting lost in, the divine mystery).
2. In order to form the habit of daily prayer with Scripture, it helps to choose a time and place where you will not be interrupted. Family members or friends could be asked to cover for you (you are "not available" for another hour or half an hour). The telephone and the doorbell will need attention.
3. On weekends, holidays or trips, special arrangements will need to be made, or perhaps simpler forms of prayer employed (the rosary, slow reading of an inspirational book, the daily "Prayer of the Church," and so on). But even in these situations one can learn how to find thirty or sixty minutes apart from others. It depends on your being determined to solve it.

4. In order to get started, seven Scripture texts to practice on (one for each day in a week) are suggested in the next point. But before launching out, please remember that it is important:
   (a) to choose one passage for each prayer period;
   (b) to stay with that one text for the whole period, whether the prayer goes well or badly;
   (c) not to shift to any other text, not to read further in the Bible than the verses indicated, nor to move restlessly from text to text; and
   (d) to let the words of Scripture work on your heart, waiting patiently for that to happen.
5. The following passages are often used to get started, but you need not feel bound by them. They are only suggestions. If you prefer some other texts of your own, by all means make use of them. (Collections of passages for prayer are never any better than "something to fall back on" when a way of praying is not clearly "given" to you—perhaps by the Holy Spirit.)

— Luke 2: 41-52 The Finding in the Temple.
— Mark 4: 35-41 The Calming of the Storm.
— Psalm 25 To You I lift up my soul, O Lord.
— Isaiah 55: 1-13 Come to the Water.
— Romans 8: 18-27 The Spirit helps us in our weakness.
— Hebrews 4: 12-16 The word of God is a two-edged sword.
— Luke 11: 1-13 Lord, teach us to pray.

It's important to make a beginning. So plunge right in! May God be with you and bless you! The Lord will not be outdone in generosity, so don't give up easily.

Chapter 2
Finding Passages in the Bible

What we've learned from centuries of actual prayer by many, many people is that shorter texts, rather than lengthy ones, work best. And not every group of verses in Scripture will serve our purpose. Large sections of the Bible, even some entire books, are not well suited to prayer.

Praying with Scripture differs from "reading the Bible," even a slow and thoughtful reading, because the traditional method we are dealing with here aims at a response of the whole person. I mean, it enables each one's entry into a personal communion with God. It takes time for a person-to-Person event to happen. But a way of reading which keeps going forward in a chapter, or over several chapters, will likely miss this aim.

What does help is to stay with a fairly short passage throughout the prayer period. By "short" I mean five or ten verses, more or less. (In a few cases like the Psalms somewhat longer is allowed, but those are exceptions.)

So the question to be faced in this chapter is how to find the right passages. In the chapter following this one we will talk about a prayer companion, someone who is in touch with good Scripture passages and can help you out with this task. But quite a few collections of prayer texts under various headings are available (I have published several of these myself). A few books of this kind are listed at the end of the chapter.

THE PRINCIPLE OF ATTRACTION

But here I'll take up the matter of which passages might be useful for you right now—as a particular person in your concrete situation. Among all the different texts given in the many collections, how can you know what texts to use today? In fact, several key signs may be noticed, and all of us need to learn how to read those signs.

It may help to recognize that a similar difficulty comes up when trying to find the right spiritual reading. I have often made the mistake of urging people to read a book that has helped me in a similar situation. But if they did take up the book they often found no strong response in themselves. What suited me turned out to be of little use to them at that time. So I've learned not to tell anyone else what to read.

Instead, I suggest they pay attention to what seems to attract them, what actually moves them when they begin to read it, and what nourishes their present needs as they go along. That's the best sign of all—the "principle of attraction," as it's often called. You are the only one who can be sure about the evidence. Does it seem to draw you? Then give it a try. Does it not hold your deeper feelings? Then put it aside and look for something else.

This is true when choosing Scripture passages as well. But let's look more closely now at what is at work here.

First of all, prayer is not in the printed words themselves. It may arise in us, of course, when we make use of them. The inspired text is only a set of black marks on a page until we read them into our minds and hearts and "prayer" begins to happen (or perhaps on a given day does not happen).

In other words, passages of Scripture—inspired by God in others, then written down and printed—are intended to be an instrument, a means to something else. Such texts are wonderfully made — they can exert a "pull" on mysterious parts of our being, somewhere deep down inside us.

The inspired words of God are the very best words to use because they are holy, strangely powerful and, as we are told in Hebrews, "living and active, sharper than any two-edged sword, piercing to the division of soul and spirit, of joints and marrow, and discerning the thoughts and intentions of the heart." [4:12]

All the same they are only instruments, and as such they need to be rightly used for their proper purpose. It's a fact that they can be poorly used, or even misused, by whoever takes them up. Why is that so? What happens when we try to pray with a text of Holy Scripture?

HOW PRAYER HAPPENS

I think the inspired words often trigger off responses in us that we don't expect. It's the unexpected event in prayer that is most important. "Graces" of prayer are gifts that come to us in a way we didn't anticipate.

And that's why I should not try to control a Scripture passage with my mind or will. This is the most common misuse of the word of God — using it to make me feel good about what I've already decided to be or to do (even if that choice of mine seems to be alright).

If the Lord chooses to console your heart, to let you feel deeply how much you are treasured and loved, you should be ready to receive that gift. Often it may be the right grace for you to pray for, too. But that's not the same as deciding that God ought to do it for you right now, or do it in the way you think it ought to be done. For you are God's servant; God is not your servant.

To put it crudely, some people imagine that their god should be stopped up in a bottle. When they have something they want this god to do, they "uncork" their bottle and set the divine power loose. And after the task is done, they want to "bottle up their god" again.

But of course the true God does not allow anything like that to happen. Those who persist in it will usually find that God has withdrawn from them. They will find themselves feeling empty and perhaps resentful because God does not choose to do what they will. (Surely we are not as crude as this? But sometimes at difficult moments we may slip into some degree of it.)

The Bible is an instrument, then, which we should not grasp too tightly. We should not try to make it do our bidding. Rather, we should let a text of Scripture work on us. We must learn how to become receivers of God's words, letting them hold us in their grip or trigger in us any movement of feeling or knowing they seek to let loose. For there are powerful mysteries in Scripture to which our hearts are somehow attuned.

As an "instrument," then, the Bible is not like a hammer or a chisel, but much more like a marvelous harp or an organ, a quiet horn or an energetic violin. And it is a musical instrument that plays to us, not one that we play to others or to ourself.

"The wind blows wherever it wills," says Jesus. "You hear the sound of it, but you do not know where it comes from or where it is going; so it is with everyone who is born of the Spirit." [Jn. 3:8]

TWO LEVELS OF AWARENESS

To see this better we should notice the two different levels to be found in everyone's awareness, an upper and a lower level. At the upper level our awareness hears words and can get the sense of them (at least on the surface). At the same level we search for and find our own words to say to others. This is where our daily conversations take place.

It is where we first receive words when we are reading, and even there our grasp of the words may be a weak one. How easily are we distracted! A shout in the street, a door slamming in the house—even a dripping faucet—can divert our attention from the text.

But we might be drawn more powerfully down into our reading whenever the text works its magic on us and pulls us into our deeper self. (In later chapters I'll be making suggestions about how to avoid the surface distractions mentioned above.)

The lower level of our awareness is where we become involved in mysterious movements of feeling and intuition. Some of these inner movements are negative or disruptive, but others may be full of peace, exciting us with desire, passionate or obscure, dull and heavy, or light and sharp.

They are extremely various, but the remarkable thing about them is that we can't directly control them very much or make them do what we want. And yet they can haunt us for a long time, or echo mysteriously in the background.

At the upper level we do have some degree of control over our thoughts and desires. We can choose the words we want to use (although sometimes we blurt out what we hadn't intended to say). We can also make up our minds, or decide to put things off, or to act and struggle perseveringly, and so on.

Often we might fail, but sometimes we do succeed. In many areas of life we may be unable to do things well, but in some special areas perhaps we have developed our technical skills and learnt how to do what others can't do.

Now, it's human to notice these two areas of awareness, the upper and the lower levels. But to be fully human is to combine them well.

If someone dwells all the time in their deeper self but is useless when it comes to practical matters, that is a one-sided person. And if others close off their deeper level of awareness in order to identify only with their technical skills, those persons too are truncated. Only when we learn how to make upper and lower levels of awareness work together can we become whole.

These facts show why praying with Scripture can be so marvellous for people today. Our technological culture makes nearly everyone grow up with a "fix" on upper-level skills. To be a success today means to become skilled in technical work—either blue-collar work or white-collar work, in building roads or machines, using computers, in medical science, repairing household gadgets, running a company, making investments, or whatever kind of skill.

Compared with people who lived in former times, nearly everyone today is a technological whiz. Even those who aren't clever with technical instruments think they ought to be. To some degree, all of us tend to become a little misshapen by this special goal of our culture. We are biased by know-how.

PRAYING WITH SCRIPTURE HELPS

And so a time set aside every day for dwelling in our lower-level awareness is literally a "god-send." It will help to pull us out of our lopsided shape and back into balance—into a sense of wholeness.

There are many other ways of doing this (including secular ways) and methods of prayer other than praying with Scripture passages, but this method is by far the most central one in our faith tradition. It is usually where to begin.

It also puts us in touch with the experience and the wisdom of our spiritual ancestors. The "passionate knowing" of Christians over many centuries of striving to live faithfully in our human world has been tested in this simple and direct method of prayer. Their wisdom was ripened by pondering over Scripture passages and this method of theirs has been handed down to us.

And so, to put it briefly, the best signs of being on the right track in your day-by-day choices of Scripture texts will be found in the responses of your own heart. You must learn now to pay close attention to what is happening deep down within yourself. Time must be given to this search. It may not come clear all at once. Keep asking the Lord to reveal to you what passages you should return to or what new passages to seek.

"Ask, and you shall receive," Jesus tells us on the subject of prayer. "Seek and you shall find. Knock, and it shall be opened to you…If you ask your father (or mother) for bread, will (s)he give you a stone?" [Mt. 7: 7,9] Certainly not! Stick with it for a while. You'll obtain what you need. This is the most basic guideline given to us by the Lord.

Practical Suggestions:

1. Many Bibles include helpful indexes at the back where lists of texts may be found under a wide range of headings.
2. For beginners, *Speak, Lord, Your Servant is Listening*, by Msgr. David E. Rosage (ISBN 1569553661) provides selections of Scripture texts for 52 weeks. Each week is given a heading. On the opposite side of each page topics on how to pray are developed.

3. Somewhat more advanced is Fr. John Veltri's *Orientations I,* revised (order from B. Broughton Co. Ltd., 2105 Danforth Ave., Toronto ON M4C 1K1 www.bbroughton.com). Several sets of very helpful themes for prayer are provided with lists of texts.
4. "Scripture Passages for Daily Prayer on the Christian Virtues" is the subtitle of my own book, *The Real Presence of the Future Kingdom* (order from Ignatian Spirituality Centre of Montreal, 4567 West Broadway, Montreal QC H4B 2A7 www.ignatiancentremtl.ca). Twelve basic virtues are each supplied with twenty-six Scripture texts for prayer.
5. It is advisable to choose one passage before beginning the prayer period—otherwise too much of your precious prayertime is lost in hunting about for a text. When you pray early in the morning, it helps to select a text the night before.
6. Once the passage has been chosen, however, you should stay with it throughout the time you've set aside for prayer. Even if the prayertime doesn't go well for you, don't move away from the passage you've chosen. Perhaps there is some reason for the difficulty you are up against. Perhaps the Lord is getting you ready for a grace of a special kind. Who knows? (And you are allowed to complain about it. Are not some of the Psalms filled with such complaints?)

   In any case, it does happen that a grace we sought for in vain during the time of prayer is received later in the day when least expected. Looking back afterwards, we see that God was preparing us during prayer (purifying our heart) for what was to come to us later on.
7. The "principle of repetition" says that we may profit from frequent returns to passages already prayed over. It depends, of course, upon several matters. When the Text in question has

served us well, we could return to it in order to renew the grace received or to follow it further into more of its meaning and value. On the other hand, we could return to a text which has proven to be difficult in order to discover what was blocking us on the previous occasion. During repetitions we could face obstacles and try to get through them.

All the same, some passages simply don't speak to us at this time in our lives (a few years from now they may hit us in the solar plexus). In general, we should mainly follow the principle of attraction and secondarily follow the principle of repetition—trying to find out what might help us to move forward.

Chapter 3
Seeing a Prayer Companion

To surrender oneself to God can be a lonely and even a rather frightening experience. At first, anyway, there seems to be something awesome and fearful about it, and perhaps this never goes away completely. That's how it is for any direct contact we may have with the divine mystery which surrounds our life.

True, we are drawn to it by our very nature. Human beings need God—just to become fully human.

And yet we tend to put off any direct meetings. Sometimes when we hear a knocking sound at the door, we don't open up. We pretend we aren't at home. For we feel alone at such moments and (let's admit it) we have a number of reasons for being afraid of God (our feelings of guilt, our shortcomings, our ignorance). What would ongoing contact with the divine mystery do to us?

That's why to be linked up with a prayer companion is a great help in more ways than one. I'll try to spell out some of these ways here.

A GOOD LISTENER

First of all, it's helpful to have someone to talk to about the religious experiences we've actually been having, some of them positive, some (perhaps) quite negative. I don't mean just anybody to talk to. It has to be a person who is used to things of that kind, knows how to take them—with a fund of sympathy and understanding to fall back on.

If we've had "a close encounter of the third kind"—somehow bumping into the divine mystery—we're sure that most other people who hear about it would think we were crazy, out of our minds, gone somewhere over the edge.

Or worse than that, they might think we are suffering from delusions. We expect to be told that we're imagining things, especially "holy" things which make us "better than others." We even tell ourselves that it would be a lot easier just to forget about it. (This has been tried, but it usually doesn't work.)

When we think this way, it's well to notice, we're taking it for granted that "others" are all hard-headed people convinced that nothing else exists in the human world but rocks, machines, money-making, debts, mosquitoes, shops loaded with goods, and the like. All those others, we fear, would be quite certain our religious experiences are unreal. We couldn't possibly let on to "them" that anything unusual (meaning, not physical) has taken place in our lives. They would be sure to laugh at us, right?

Not necessarily. In point of fact, this conviction is for the most part mistaken. According to Abraham Maslow, the prominent U.S. psychologist, "peak" experiences need attention in people's lives. At first he thought only a few persons had them. But later investigations proved that he had badly underestimated the facts. Nearly everyone, he found, has peak experiences, and some have quite a few of them in their lifetime.

Besides, the attitudes in the world around us (dating several decades back) that used to make it embarrassing to talk about such happenings have changed since then. More recently it has become much less surprising, almost normal, to mention the experiences one has of "supernatural" events. To value one's spiritual side (even if only in a secular sense) has become an accepted attitude today in a surprising number of people.

In any case, few doubt that the depths of the human spirit have an important influence on all we do. And deep experiences of a religious kind can't simply be explained away in terms of physical objects and sensations. There are, of course, people who continue to think that way, but they are much fewer than they used to be. That's why prayer companions are not so hard to find these days.

By the term "prayer companion" I mean people who have already been through at least several years (usually longer) of spiritual direction in their own lives. They have prayed with Scripture passages and gotten in touch with their experiences of God. They've learned how to speak about their own deep movements of religious feeling. They've come to know something about the rich lore handed down to us on matters of this kind.

What they've received has been precious to them. They've recognized what a difference it makes to have someone to talk to who is familiar with such things. And they feel called to make that gift available to others who are in need of it.

More important still, they have learned how to listen to others. They can receive with respect the attempts by others to put into words what has been taking place deep within. They know how to help other persons express their experiences of God.

All that's needed in order to be linked up with a prayer companion is a desire to know God better. It isn't necessary to have had "big" experiences or to be in the middle of a crisis. Perhaps there is too much talk about "crises" these days. What is much more common are moments of growth, obstacles met, longings felt which God seems to be putting in our heart, and a desire to learn how to pray on a daily basis.

DEEP LISTENING

In the second place, I would mention the dangers of isolation and the human value of another's response to what is taking place in us. Since we are social by nature, whatever happens to us needs to be shared. If we never speak of our experiences, their meaning tends to fade, and their worth diminishes or even seems unreal. This is so, I believe, for every important experience that we have.

For example, if I've been disturbed by a bad dream, I could decide to tell nobody about it, to bottle it up inside myself until the negative feelings it's giving me begin to quiet down. Fear of seeming like a fool or of giving myself away by letting others know my weaknesses could prevent me from dealing with the dream and its message to myself.

Besides, if I'm not used to talking about dreams, it's quite likely that I'll take them the wrong way. I'll form a distorted view of what my dreams are trying to say to me, and I'll bury a false version deep down inside myself. Obviously, it will tend to limit me further and do me harm. My energies get tied up in something false.

But the dream might come much clearer if I could find someone to share it with. Usually another person (especially someone who's used to this) can see the point of my dream better than I can myself. Why is that so? It seems to be because we need to stand outside our own minds (outside what I've called our "upper-level awareness") in order to get the real point of dreams.

The same is true of what "comes" to us unexpectedly in times of prayer with Scripture passages.

Is it wrong for me to compare prayer events with dreams? I don't think so. Even ordinary daydreams are often made use of by God to draw us forward. But when we put time aside for prayer (particularly prayer done with texts of Holy Scripture), the images, words, and the movements of inner feelings that come to us then are very similar in kind to the "messages" sent to us from our deeper selves during times of sleep.

HUMAN LITTLENESS

And it is normal for this sort of thing to happen. Our limited circle of human awareness is surrounded by mystery. This is true for everyone, not just for those who believe in God. It's part of our human situation to be unsure of where we are going, uncertain of what will happen to us each day.

Our usual sense of self (no matter how talented and educated we are) is of being "in between" our past self and what lies before us in the future. We usually feel unfinished to some degree or other. At least, that's what I've learned from many persons who have opened their inner lives to me, and it's what I've often felt within myself.

In other words, our littleness can be known each day, and can be tasted whenever we get into a moment of self-awareness. Many people in our culture try to hide this fact from themselves and especially from others. But I think nearly everyone has feelings of that kind from time to time.

Striving to be successful, or at least to be effective and to be recognized by others as well organized — this urgent effort imposed on us by our society as we grow up makes us want to deny our ordinary littleness. And so the weakness and ignorance that's part of what we know about ourselves doesn't get expressed.

What a relief, then, to find someone who already knows these facts by personal experience and is willing to listen to us! Someone who affirms our worth in God's sight in spite of this. That's what a prayer companion does for us. When we speak about experiences which occurred when praying with Scripture passages, a prayer companion knows how to receive them rightly. It's a person who listens deeply.

Now, "deep" listening is a skill that comes with practice. It means giving the other person time, asking questions patiently until the matter comes clear, and feeding back ways of speaking about it which come from our spiritual tradition.

Can you remember the first time another person listened to you "deeply"? Have you received that gift from another already? It's a wonderful feeling, as many have told me. More than that, it can make us more human, more free, and able to move forward in dealing with whatever we are facing at the time.

DISCERNING TRUE FROM FALSE

There's a final reason for needing another person to talk to about the spiritual experiences we've been having. This has to do with the question whether they are true or false experiences, right or wrong. Are they perhaps illusions and deceptions? Or are they the real thing? We need to know, and we'd like to find ways of coming to solid conclusions on such a key question.

The more traditional way of putting this is as follows: Do our spiritual experiences come from God or are they from the Enemy (from the Evil One)? Are they perhaps just our own inventions? And how can we know for sure? Perhaps what is happening in us can be explained psychologically? That question, too, has to be faced. Let's try to sort some of this out.

PSYCHOLOGY AND FAITH

It's quite true that psychological explanations can be given and to a certain extent would be valid. Besides, it's often helpful to look at events from the psychic point of view. That need not throw us off. We should be ready to take psychological questions into account.

But there are two further points to be made. The first point is that psychological views are limited: They can't give us anything like a total explanation. The second point is that just as in other fields of knowledge, the psychological field is being dug into by many different specializations, many of which disagree with the others. There are plenty of different opinions.

My first point says that, while psychology can legitimately be applied to everything (including religion, of course), it always comes from a limited point of view. It looks at every part of human life from the viewpoint of the individual psyche. That is a good thing to do in itself. But there are several other points of view which are equally valid (for example, medical and sociological) and psychology can't possibility replace those others. Least of all can it replace religious faith, which looks at human life in its relationship with God.

The second point is that there are many different explanations in depth psychology. In fact, there are lots of theories, plenty of opposed schools of thought. Unfortunately, there are also too many "pop" psychologists ready to practice on their friends. The poet Alexander Pope wrote, "a little knowledge is a dangerous thing."

New psychological "theories" and self-help books are constantly being marketed in response to a seemingly insatiable hunger for quick fixes. Many earlier authors are treated with disdain by those who come after them. But we notice that like other popular fads, they tend to fall by the wayside.

I'm sure you're familiar with this kind of thing in the world today. It always occurs where competition is intense for a share of the market. But the same holds true for people's low feeling about themselves, their sense of weakness, their neediness of spirit, their hopes for some remedy or other. Cheap solutions are noisily promoted and first class workers in psychology suffer from all this. They know that real progress in handling personal problems take time. There are no quick fixes.

Patient efforts to get at the facts will be needed. A sense of human limitations and of the limited point of view of our own contributions are just as important. If someone needs professional help from a psychiatrist, prayer should not be put forward as a replacement for that. On the other side, neither should psychology be touted as a good substitute for faith.

Prayer companions, as I'm using the term here, are persons aware of these facts. They are trained to listen carefully to the desires and faith experiences of those who believe in God. They also know the difference between the viewpoint of faith and the viewpoint of depth psychologies.

They don't try to pose as psychic healers. They send people back to the Lord in prayer, giving them Scripture passages which might be helpful in particular cases. And they patiently stay with each one's efforts to find the truth or falsehood of prayer experiences. They know what our age-old tradition teaches us about how to discern the truth or falsehood, the meaning and value of what happens in a life of faith. They help those they accompany to learn the same methods for themselves.

In a later chapter I will go into much more detail on the topic of spiritual discernment. That is a crucial skill to acquire, but several other matters will need attention before we get to that subject.

Practical Suggestions

1. In most neighborhoods today at least a few spiritual directors can be found. In some areas a larger number are available. Elsewhere they might still be rather scarce. But more and more opportunities for training spiritual directors, and I mean not only clergy, sisters and brothers (or monks and nuns in monasteries), but single or married lay persons as well. If you are hoping to find a prayer companion, you should ask around for names of spiritual directors who live within a reasonable range of your home. You can also consult the web site of Spiritual Directors International at www.sdiworld.org, which maintains a directory of certified spiritual directors and prayer companions.

    In this book I am using the term "prayer companion" to mean a spiritual director who coaches beginners how to pray daily with Scripture passages, how to keep a prayer journal and how to express faith experiences and seek to discern them. A prayer companion is a spiritual director who helps another person to get started with daily prayer.

2. My advice is not to lock yourself onto a particular prayer companion right away. There is a sort of "chemistry" between any two persons that must be taken into account. Make an appointment and go to see the companion who may have been recommended to you, but wait awhile before deciding to ask for a regular series of meetings. In other words, make it a single appointment until you feel right about the other person. After all, what you are looking for is a week-by-week set of meetings in which you will gradually learn to speak about the faith experiences you are having. The kind of sharing involved will not become possible until you trust each other.

So you should not go forward if you don't feel you could trust the prayer companion you are meeting for the first time.

3. Of course, you have the right to expect complete confidentiality on the part of the prayer companion. All spiritual direction depends entirely upon the director's faithful keeping of the directee's confidence. It is understood, then, without saying anything about it, that whatever you share together, whatever you reveal about yourself, will never be repeated anywhere else, not even indirectly hinted at.

   You may take this for granted, then, but today it is better to bring the subject up. Many trained spiritual directors and prayer companions will save you the worry by mentioning it themselves. They will give you definite assurances that your confidence will be carefully respected.

4. The other side of this, of course, is your own perseverance in being faithful to your commitments. You will be expected to find time to pray every day and to give this high priority. You will also need to keep a regular prayer journal, as directed, and turn up faithfully at weekly appointments with your director. When the going gets tough (you run into obstacles, or your companion is asking difficult questions, and so on), you will need to soldier on with considerable maturity.

5. All the same, your relationship with a prayer companion is a free one. That means that you always have the right to withdraw from it or to bring it to an end. Usually this should be worked out explicitly with the prayer companion.

   Sometimes it may be the companion who suggests closure—that your daily prayer with Scripture has borne fruit, that you are well on your way, and that it's time for you to be on your own again—in order to avoid any kind of false dependency.

Chapter 4
Keeping Troubles at a Distance

By now it should be clear that praying with Scripture texts is an activity that differs quite a lot from other things people do in the course of a normal day. In this sense, it has a frame around it. We step through that frame into another space. We enter a different dimension. And after a short while (30 to 60 minutes), we return to our ordinary life again—hopefully, feeling refreshed.

It differs from other types of action by being so receptive, so centered in the deep self, and focused so directly on the divine mystery. But it can do this only because struggles of our daily life are removed to some extent from our attention. Getting a certain "distance" from daily concerns is what I want to discuss in this chapter. Why is it needed? And how does it work? (As we'll see, it's a special skill that can grow into an acquired habit.)

First, then, it's needed urgently because the secular, technological society which we all inhabit, when allowed to become all-important and all-consuming for us, neglects the faith dimension, the mystery of life, the "beyond" that calls us endlessly. If we are just going through the motions of a Christian life externally and in fact giving our main attention to the pursuit of momentary pleasures and the rat-race of consumption and competition, then the deep-down emptiness of our lives will soon make itself felt.

Even a person committed to hard work in a worthwhile job, as long as the faith-dimension is excluded, will inevitably, I think, feel a certain "flatness" and loss of value. Something is missing—a lack of appreciation by others (or by oneself)? Or feelings of being cut-off and misunderstood? We wonder what's the matter. Could we try to respond to this gnawing void by denial? Or by running faster? Or by plunging into more self-indulgence? Or by anger and resentment? All those evasions only cook up a pretty thin soup for the hungry human heart. There can be no real help for us other than a direct entry into the presence of the divine mystery. For Christians, a method of daily prayer with Scripture passages can open the door to that adventure.

But is this "getting away from things" like going on a brief vacation every day? Yes and no. Both prayer and a vacation aim to refresh us and enable us to return to daily tasks with a renewed spirit, true enough. Both are similar in that they put a kind of distance between ourselves and what we do every day. But on a vacation we usually leave home. The distance is geographical. In daily prayertimes, on the other hand, the distance is not physical but directly psychic.

For times of prayer we may choose a special space in our home, but that's as far as we need to travel. The space-frame we want to step through is "located" wherever we are when we decide to pray. As in C. S. Lewis's Tales of Narnia, a secret entrance may be found in our own house—perhaps in a cupboard.

It's best to have a regular place to pray where we won't be interrupted by others or become too distracted by surrounding events (a few suggestions on this are given below). But whatever the physical set-up one may use, its aim is to get psychic distance from activities and relationships that occupy most of our attention before and after the prayertime.

In every case, in order to get into interior prayer, a first preparatory step is to move away from ordinary events. It's essential to distance ourselves from our daily occupations in the sense of "being beyond their reach" for awhile. But why is this needed? Wouldn't it be better to pray directly about our daily troubles? Shouldn't we ask for divine help in what we're actually doing?

THE MOUNTAIN AND THE DESERT

It's a well-known fact in our spiritual tradition that efforts to connect directly with divine reality have usually involved a separation from social life by going up a mountain or by withdrawing into a desert region. That's how Moses first met the one true God at his famous "burning bush" episode. [Exod.3:1-14] Many stories of the great prophets of Israel tell of similar moments of isolation from the busy world.

Jesus himself goes out to meet John the Baptist in the desert. [Lk. 3:2b; Mt. 3: 13]. Later, at key moments in his life, he climbs a mountain in order to pray with the Father—apart from his disciples. [Mt. 14:23] For Christians, Mount Tabor and the Mount of Olives are special places for this reason alone. [Mt. 17:1; Lk. 22:39-41] And Jesus wants us to do the same: "When you pray, go to your room, close the door, and pray to your Father, who is unseen." [Mt. 6:6a]

Similar stores are told of the saints and mystics. But the need that's implied is put into practice at more ordinary times as well and in the lives of ordinary believers. It's also what "retreats" are meant to make possible for busy lay parishioners.

On the first evening of weekend retreats, I've often said to the group of tired-looking persons who have managed to get away from their usual commitments, "The Lord has invited us to 'come apart and rest awhile.' And here we are on a little mountain top…" (or words to that effect). "At the end of your retreat," I tell them, "you'll be returning to your tasks in the 'valley' below, but in the meantime you can let those burdens go and be alone with God."

This doesn't mean that Christ is not to be found in the world of daily events—of course he is! Nor does it mean that he doesn't join us in our usual activities. The divine Lord certainly seeks to do that, and to do it much more effectively than at present.

According to St. Ignatius, we should learn how to "find God in all things"—to become contemplative in action.

What it does mean, though, is that action is not everything and that if we try to pray only in times of action we'll soon lose any sense of the depth dimension. Our spiritual tradition is very clear on this point. If we want to become united more securely to God in our active lives, then we'll need to add to our activities regular times of prayer apart from action.

This may seem like a contradiction, but it's not really. It's a deep and important truth about the effects of the busy world on human beings like us. (It's also true that if we neglect to put our faith into action our prayer will soon become unreal. But that's the flip side of the story, which we'll return to later.)

Life isn't simple. Different gifts, each of them valuable in themselves, usually have to be balanced by other gifts. If they're not countered in this fashion, they'll likely get thrown out of kilter. And a good example of this truth can be found in relating prayer to action. It isn't enough to stress a life of faith-filled actions. In fact, it's foolish to talk about prayer as if it could survive as prayer done in the midst of activities alone. (Maybe it could for a while, but not for long.)

Our direct contact with the divine mystery in prayer is valuable in itself, but it's also valuable because it connects us with what matters most in our active life. Without the times of prayer apart from actions, we easily lose the divine connection during the actions themselves.

No, our tradition is unanimous in insisting that our active life, however filled with prayer, should be accompanied by separate times of prayer every day, a kind of prayer in which there will be leisure for one-to-one communion at a deep level with the divine mystery.

PRAYER OF COMMUNION

It's not enough to make prayers of petition, either. Of course we should be asking for what we need. St. Ignatius (a great master of the art of prayer for active people) insists on petition prayers being carefully done.

In fact, he says we should try to get more and more light about exactly what grace we need at present. When we know what our precise need is, then we ought to ask for it trustingly and persistently. Pray with complete confidence that you're going to get what you seek. But petitions of this kind are not the only kind of prayer we need.

What we need as well is prayer of communion. There's a deep call in us to a personal way of relating individually with God. And that call comes from the Lord himself: "Make your home in me," Jesus tells his disciples, "as I make my home in you." [Jn. 15:4]

Elsewhere he speaks like this: "Believe in God and believe in me. There are many rooms in my Father's house, and I am going to prepare a place for you. I would not tell you this if it were not so. And after I go and prepare a place for you, I will come back and take you to myself, so that you will be where I am." [Jn. 14:1-3]

This invites us to a personal communion (a mysterious, deep kind of union at a person-to-person level). We may not be able to explain this exactly, but I think most people know what it's all about. We have a longing for it, and when it's been given us we feel fulfilled by it. We are refreshed in spirit because we seldom receive enough of it in our busy lives. Praying with Scripture passages is one of the best ways of entering into the divine presence in union with Jesus Christ. It makes a prayer of communion, as I've been calling it, easier to receive. It tends to get us ready for a deeper kind of personal union with God to be given us.

THE TWO SELVES

There are not only two levels of awareness in us but also two kinds of self. In the last chapter I stressed the difference between the upper and lower levels of our inner experience, and I think every reflective person already knows how they differ. Now I want to add to this the centers of selfhood which belong at each level.

At the upper level, where our five senses bring us awareness of the outer world and where we interact with other persons in our social life, the "I" or "me" that each of us feels to be involved may be named the "conscious self." This center of self-awareness (the psychologists tend to call it the "ego," but I'd prefer to avoid that term) is very important to us. It's the part of myself that's actively engaged in the outer world. It's where I normally "live."

In order to live effectively in human societies, a healthy conscious self will have to arise in us. Adolescence is the stage of life when we try to achieve an independent self of this sort. Easy for some, it's quite a trial for many others. As we move beyond the adolescent stage we become able to earn a living on our own, to make decisions about marriage, about work, and about the social lifestyle we prefer. We become responsible for our own lives, and it's our conscious self that makes this possible. Nobody's perfect, of course, and that means that our conscious self usually has a number of shortcomings. Some are too aggressive, others too timid. Some are fearfully uncertain and others painfully shallow. Tensions are dominant in some cases, but illusions prop up a sagging self in others.

Whatever the defects may be, they're usually focused upon the problems in each one's life situation, and these problems vary a lot. They can be difficulties in work, in income, in dealing with others, in marrying, in studies and exams, in settling down, in making real commitments or finding a place to live. Several more could be mentioned, and all of them involve emotional reactions. These are problems in our social life that are mainly faced by our conscious self.

But there's much more to the self than what lies on the surface of social awareness. We might say that our selfhood looks outward but also looks inward. In fact, there are two opposite poles to what we feel about ourself: there's an upper-level pole and a lower-level pole. If the first of these has been named the conscious self, the second may be called the "inner self."

To test this out, reflect a moment on daydreaming. Often this happens when we're doing monotonous chores—stacking dishes, being bored during meetings, digging up the garden, driving in easy traffic. While continuing to manage the task at hand, our mind (which isn't busy enough) tends to drift off on a tangent…going who knows where? Sometimes we stumble into interesting scenery.

Now, what's going on at such moments? Clearly, the conscious self-center has been put on automatic pilot, and this sets the inner self free to wander. More than that, this inner center of self can receive our main attention. It isn't responding to events in our social world (the monotony of our habitual tasks takes care of that). Rather, it's opening to uncontrolled dramas, memories or fantasies. Any stray image seems to invite the inner self to rove at random—or to feel propelled by desires.

What it illustrates is the wealth of the inner world into which all of us may be invited. When we seek prayer of communion and make use of our imaginations with the help of Scripture passages, we are taking advantage of this interior realm. We are exploring the spiritual world which is our birthright.

PRAYER AND PROBLEM SOLVING

There are many hungers in the human heart, many desires that can't be satisfied by the merely physical events in our social world: buying more food, more gadgets, more clothing, or playing games, doing exercise, plunging into work over our heads, even running away from what we feel deep down—none of this will get rid of what I call "the Big Ache" that reasserts its power, again and again, in the depth of our being. Only God can satisfy the Big Ache of the human soul. I think everybody knows this fact, even though not everyone will acknowledge or act on it.

We may try to lock the Big Ache away and concentrate instead on solving problems in the world outside us. If I should become famous, would that do it? Not likely. If I won a giant lottery and spend money furiously, could I find satisfaction that way? All the evidence is against it. What about a mad love affair, getting into a "magnificent obsession"? It wouldn't help for very long. At some point down the road you'd have to face the wreckage of your life and take responsibility for the real choices you've been making.

When we travel (when we try to run away to another place), an ancient poet tells us, we always take ourselves along with us. At the other end of our journey we will find the inner pole of our discontent still at hand. In other words, no matter where you go, there you are. If unresolved difficulties of that sort call urgently for attention, it would perhaps be better to deal with them at home, before we leave.

For beyond problem solving comes the meaning and value of all we do. At a deeper level than mundane or routine tasks lurks the inner self, who seeks worthwhile aims, desires justice, hopes to become lost in unselfish goals and to find a meaningful life at last.

Even "happiness" and "self-fulfillment" turn out to be empty aims if we seek them for their own sake. But they might be rich if our happiness results from forgetting our self in jobs worth doing and if our self-fulfillment means being pulled beyond our limited abilities by divine grace.

In sum, then, a whole lifetime of problem solving (very good in itself) won't satisfy the Big Ache in our hearts. And on the other side, a total devotion to our inner selves won't lead to contentment and fulfillment. What's missing in both cases is the involvement of our deepest hearts in the divine mystery beyond ourselves.

That's what prayer of communion brings about. It calls us away from our problems and our troubles, it unites us interiorly with God in Christ and transforms us by means of that union, and then it sends us back into the troublesome and problematic world. But more and more we will return to our daily tasks not only refreshed, but also (at least a little) different from what we were before.

Praying with Scripture, then, is the very opposite of problem solving. In order to get into this kind of prayer, we need to learn how to distance ourselves psychically from our daily concerns. When that's done well, we find that our inner selves become available to make a direct connection with the Lord who loves us, calls us, and connects us with the One who is beyond all.

Practical Suggestions:

1. The time for praying with Scripture passages should not be when you are tired and unable to do anything else. In those times you'll likely fall asleep. It's better not to "force yourself into prayer" against the grain. Instead, try to find a daily time when you can relax and enjoy some deep communing with God. Everyone should give high priority to moments of that kind.

   Often the best time for prayer is early in the morning, but some individuals are at their worst then (several belts of strong coffee only bring them to the edge of human awareness). Others pray during their noon break from work (they enjoy being alone then). Others find time and protection after getting home and before supper. A few others can pray in the evening or before going to bed. It depends on your daily pattern, your "biorhythm," and you are the best judge of that.

2. The place also needs attention. Some prefer a church or chapel that's convenient for them. Others have prepared a little corner in their house: they use a prie-dieu, a chair, a crucifix or holy picture, perhaps a prayer candle to light up, or incense to burn, or whatever they find helpful.

   Others again are forced to drive somewhere else to find a quiet place. Some go to a park in summer, or stay in their heated car in colder weather.

   On longer trips away from home, especially when visiting with others, the physical setting for daily prayer may be quite diverse. Sitting in a moving bus or plane, walking on the beach at dawn, seeking out a garden or a bower in the woods; maybe even stranger places will prove to be useful for those who have formed the habit of getting a psychic distance from events in the world around them. (There are further skills to learn beyond "getting away from our usual burdens." Information on those skills will be found in the next two chapters.)

3. Psychic distance from your daily concerns (I mean, not just false anxieties but normal responsibilities—your work, your family relationships and your friends, etc.) can be achieved quickly when you've formed the habit of tuning out from your surroundings:

    (a) reduce your awareness of the conscious self to a pilot light: since this is what you do when falling asleep at night, you already "know" (at least indirectly) how to do this; but for prayer you need a little awareness—enough to read the text of Scripture and to stay awake (our next chapter will show how to focus this attention on the presence of the Lord);

    (b) in order to attend exclusively on the words of the passage chosen, letting them become active in your mind and heart, you must let go your direct concerns about social life and become as receptive as you can (passive, but also interested in what might come); one way to handle a more persistent worry is to focus on it distinctly, imagine that you hang it up in a cupboard, and close the cupboard door; then re-enter your receptive space.

4. This means that our usual habits of problem solving can be set aside for a short time. It applies, not only to technical difficulties, but also to mental questions—for example, points of doctrine, intellectual questions that people raise against the faith, moral teachings and solutions to practical issues in our world. All these matters, no matter how important they may be at other times, are simply distractions during prayer of communion with the Lord.

The best method for handling such preoccupations is to step aside from them. Don't try to argue with them (arguing gives them too much of your energy). Don't become involved with them in any way. Just duck your head and let them sail past. Ignore them and calmly take up the sacred words again. (Put yourself back into God's presence, and return to your inner sense of self—more on this later.)

5. You should patiently practice these acts of withdrawal from outer stimuli (sensations or problems) and of returning to the form of prayer you are learning, repeating this over and over until the habit of doing so begins to form. Some will take to this like a duck to water. Others will need to work at it for a considerable time. Most are somewhere between these extremes, and only need patience in finding the receptivity needed.

There is an art to getting psychic distance, but there are also skills that can be learned by means of a little persistence. Each individual may have to give special attention to one or another skill. A prayer companion can be quite helpful in suggesting ways of doing so to a particular person.

Here is a saying to keep in mind: "When getting ready to pray, all your activity should go to make yourself passive."

Chapter 5: Entering into God's Presence (and staying there)

Our way of being in someone's "presence" can vary a good deal. Partly it depends on how much attention is being given to the other person. But there is also the ability to "dwell" in another's heart, becoming aware of an inward centering of our own that makes us human subjects—who can receive a similar gift.

The reason is that, if you can't realize yourself humanly as a subject, then you aren't easily going to stay in the heart of another person (dwelling in that other "subject"). And the other person won't easily be present to you in the same way.

The notations of "presence" and of "subject" are connected here. But let's look at them one at a time.

BEING PRESENT TO ANOTHER PERSON

The sharpest feeling I can get of what this means may come to me when someone else doesn't pay much attention to what I'm saying. That person isn't being "present" to me, and it bothers me to be ignored and neglected, or misunderstood. "Will you please pay attention? You're not listening! You haven't heard a thing I said!" Usually complaints like these were made to us by our parents or other grown-ups when we were little, and we realized that our mind had drifted off to something else. We "came back" into the room with a jolt and perhaps gave our attention much better to what our mother (or whoever) was trying to tell us—at least until we became distracted again.

Perhaps we began our life without too much sense of focus and with a vaguely shifting attention. We had to learn how to fix our whole mind on a single outside source of information—and keep it there until what we were seeing and hearing was completely taken in. This was a skill most of us had to acquire. It wasn't born with us.

But it's different when, as grown-ups ourselves, we suffer from another's lack of attention. In some situations this can hurt. We resent it because it seems like an absence of caring on the other person's part. The other knows how to be present, but doesn't want to do so right now.

That person may love me, but I'm not receiving any benefit from it. Despite my need of attention at this very moment, that person is wandering off somewhere else. The other's mind and heart are far away from me, and I don't know why. At times that be hard for me to accept.

Being distracted, then, is the very opposite of being present. Being present means to give my whole attention to another person, and being distracted means to leave at least some of it elsewhere. Why do we get distracted? Well, because another point of interest pulls us away, or perhaps because we are beginning to lose interest in what we at first began to see and hear with full attention.

So, what exactly does this "being present" mean? Obviously, it's much more than two persons being in the same room at the same time. But, then, what is the extra part of it? Is it merely paying attention or listening carefully, or being sympathetic? Those are certainly important, but I believe much more is needed. As a way to suggest what's involved, I'd like to propose the image of being "tuned in" to each other.

REACHING ATTUNEMENT

Paying strict attention isn't enough. A person who treats you as an enemy could pay very close attention to what you're doing and saying in order to undermine you better. When another is attacking us, we tend to watch and listen carefully. But that's not the kind of "presence" we're interested in here.

Yet this is how some people actually feel about God (they may not be fully aware of it). They imagine God as watching them — the Great Eye in the sky — and not at all in a friendly way, either. God is keeping close tabs on what they do and say, even on how they think and feel, in order to punish them (so they assume) when the right time comes.

To a certain degree they are alienated from this "God" who is so ready to judge them harshly or pounce on them as soon as they fall into sin or make a mistake. And who could blame them for disliking such a being? It's a false image of God, of course. In fact, it's a wicked idol that's been substituted, in their experience, for the true God revealed to us by Jesus in the Gospels.

Just how this and other false images of God became so widely accepted in our culture is too long a story to get into here. At least it could be said that puritanical warps of this kind have been around for some time now and still influence far too many people.

In getting rid of those warps, it won't help to go to the other extreme and paint the divine mystery as a sort of namby-pamby Santa Claus who winks at every evil, doesn't care about oppression, suffering, hypocrisy and murder, preferring to give out chocolates and butterscotch sundaes. If that's what being sympathetic means, then it has nothing to do with the true God of Christian faith.

Sympathy is important and it can be given a good meaning, but that will require a whole context of truths about human beings, what they need, where they come from and where they're going, what choices they are making, what their life is about... All of those facts call for respect if we are to become sympathetic in a helpful, creative sense.

As a result, attentiveness, careful listening and sympathy can be excellent gifts to receive, even essential ones. But by themselves they can't tell us what it means to be "present" to another person in the sense intended here. That will call for an ongoing care for the larger situation of the other, the personal history, the relationships, the struggles and the growth that is still in progress (still unfinished). It means being clued into that person's concrete life as a whole.

To bring all those matters into a single awareness will need a lot of continued openness. It will take time to get "attuned" to the other's special ways, current obstacles and long-term possibilities. It will also include a desire for the other person's growth.

Time will be needed for this because human beings don't reveal themselves all at once. Sometimes they don't even know themselves very well, so how could they tell us what it means or what its value might be?

Believing in our own goodness usually comes about only with the help of others—who believe in us despite our shortcomings of the moment. And since external habits, even quite off-putting ones, may partly be defenses which serve to keep others away from our hidden troubles, it will take time to recognize walls and barricades—and to see through them to what's on the other side.

Believing in others' true selves, and hoping for their growth to what is better always calls for an amazing attunement to their created goodness. This is how we find our Lord approaching us and relating to us when we experience his presence during prayer on Gospel texts. He looks at us with compassionate love. It's a very rare thing to receive from another person.

He joins himself to me, in particular, with a faithful, ongoing commitment. He treats me as an individual whom he believes in and for whom he has great hopes. In a few words, he is attuned to me from the start.

This is such an unexpected gift that many are utterly floored by it when they first receive it. We don't even have to deserve it! How could we possibly earn, not only so much respect, but such a unique attunement to our inmost selves? How could another feel what we're like even better than we do ourselves?

To be "attuned" here means taking into account all the facts of our life, but also how we've adapted ourselves to those facts (in their concreteness) as we struggle to deal with them. Besides this, it means getting into harmony with the best that might realistically be felt about us. As a result, the worst is filtered out like so much static, and the true theme with all its undertones and its insistent heartbeat comes through.

Whenever another person gives me that kind of focused and in-depth attention, I am changed by it. That other person is present to me—and I know what "being present" can mean in this context—it means being loved. Perhaps we can remember having received that kind of attention from our mother when we were tiny, and perhaps we've felt the loss of it later on, after we've moved beyond her reach.

Then, as grown-ups, when a similar gift is given us by a lover or a true friend, it's like coming home after a long absence. It's like finding our true self again. (For some grown-ups it might be for the first time ever.)

In order to give the same gift to others, then, we'll have to learn how to focus our attention on them as unique, as having their own history of growth that will take time for us to understand. Going through all of that personal history might enable us to imagine where they've come from and where they desire to go.

Learning how to love another person in this way will not be easy to do on our own. It calls for a double deepening, a deeper sense of our own worth and an ability to sense and to believe in the other's deep gifts—both of these at once. Usually we need a first-class community to bring that out in us (a richly endowed family or parish or set of friendships). And communities of that sort don't simply grow on trees. They are graced by God.

THE REAL PRESENCE

In the Middle Ages the Christian sense of the risen Lord's divine presence in the faith-community was experienced most powerfully in the Eucharist. That may seem natural to us today, but I think it was not usual in the earliest times and grew up gradually in the Church over several centuries (especially from the 5th to the 10th, A.D.).

Those times were called "Dark Ages" because of the widespread breakdown of social order in a civilized sense that people endured then. It meant a hard life for nearly everyone. The Lord was not felt to be near in institutions or communities, and so his presence became more richly experienced in the Eucharist (at Mass and Holy Communion).

Compared to what was their lot in the outer world of sensations and social conflicts (so much oppression, pillage, robbery, murder, and so little peace, justice, protection), the inner world of communion with God in Christ seemed to be very consoling. The point for us is: those interior experiences were much more "real" than what was going on all around them in the world.

Of course, most human beings (then, as now) were given up to gross sensations, to pleasure-seeking and to flee from pain at any cost. But those who sought to be united with God could come to experience a true life in contrast to the false life met in their surroundings. The Lord made himself present to them, and this was a "real" presence compared to the unreality of what they met in the outer world.

Maybe most of us today feel things are inverted. The outer world of sense experiences, manufactured goods, scientific inventions, the Internet and so on, may seem to be utterly real compared to the inner feelings known to us through faith. What we come to know in prayer may have a much lesser "reality" for us because of our situation today in modern culture.

But on the other side of the scale we may also find unreality in the world of the electronic media, in advertising claims (full of distorted truths, as we know), and in the inflated egotism of public figures. Add to this the sense of emptiness, so often mentioned today, the lack of true purpose and meaning, in the hyped-up activities and super-salesmanship of a consumer society. Technology often seems to highlight the unreality of life for many people in our culture. What is the point of existence? Where will it all end?

Only our contact with the divine reality through faith and hope may bring some degree of confidence that our "life project" will become worthwhile. And that contact may be felt whenever God is present to our experience.

When I was a child, I felt God's presence in Holy Communion, and by extension I tried to reach it during "visits to the Tabernacle," where the divine Son was living in our midst and could be prayed to in a very personal way. That's how I was taught as a small boy, and I think this was typical for most Roman Catholics prior to Vatican II.

But notice that this focused my attention upon the "Real Presence" of Christ in the Eucharist—outside myself (inside only during the moments of Communion). All the same, the larger truth ought to include the community of those who believe, the faith community of people who (through the actions of an ordained priest) bring the Eucharist into being.

The Real Presence of the risen Lord is given to the community first of all. Otherwise it couldn't be realized at Mass times in the Eucharist (and later reserved in the Tabernacle). It's a common experience, and yet all the members can feel the Lord's nearness individually—deep within their own being.

The consoling words at the close of Matthew's Gospel, "I will be with you always, even to the end of time" [Mt. 28:20b], were spoken to the community of believers and was not restricted to the Eucharist. For Jesus says elsewhere, "Whenever two or three are gathered in my name, there I am in their midst." [Mt. 18:20]

To sum up, then, the sense of our own reality can best become known when others make their presence to us strongly felt. But its deeper Christian reality has been handed down to us in our devotional tradition: the divine Son is really present in our faith communities, and we can feel this Reality in our hearts.

These interior experiences were given to us in our faith tradition. Early in the twentieth century, devotion to the Real Presence of Christ was renewed in the Church. This explains my boyhood experiences (already mentioned) of union with Christ in Holy Communion and during visits to the Blessed Sacrament.

But in recent decades the whole sense of this has been changing in remarkable ways (although many cling to their older habits despite all difficulties). But what it means may be grasped, I believe, only by going into the matter of being "a subject," which is my second main topic here.

PERSONAL SUBJECTS

Today much more attention is being given to our ways of relating to one another. Human beings always had relationships of many different kinds, of course. But what is new for us is the growing focus on persons—for their own sake. As a result, there has come about a remarkably intense awareness of one's inner self, and the name for this is "the human subject." (For a few groups in earlier times these matters were already well known, but more recently they became much more widespread—they affected many more people—and that's what makes the difference.)

I've said above that an individual becomes a human "subject" when an inner centering has taken place which enables that person to respond to others from much greater depths of self-awareness. One of the main results of this event can be the sense of personal changes in one's life, of choices to be made, of what results (for example) from accepting another's gift of love. It involves a lot! It will certainly lead to much more and make me into a different kind of person.

Just how this inner centering comes about will be considered in the next chapter, but here I'd like to note that the "inner self" is not a fixed thing. It's mysterious. It can change and develop. Unexpected new powers are sometimes awakened and released in it.

And it isn't even an "it." It's a he or a she. Often it's more like a "them"—many-sided and different from what I usually think about myself (about my conscious self). "How could I have answered the way I did?"—I find myself wondering. Or "why did I do that?" There seems to be more than one of me.

When we are young adults, we're usually working hard to find our "identity." Exactly what kind of a person am I going to become? That can be quite a puzzle. But then, just when we imagine we've got it solved, the inner centering we've received tends to trigger off new desires that don't fit the self we thought we were.

If we can get over our fear and shock at this, and if we come to feel more peaceful about these new powers in ourselves, then a whole new future begins to open up for us. For we are human subjects in a creative way. The values we seek will make a big difference for the kind of person we become. And we're able to make key choices on such matters during our lifetime. In a spiritual sense, we can perform a sort of "genetic surgery" on ourselves.

Naturally, each of us is not alone in all this. No one becomes a human subject in isolation from others. Only in groups does it happen in the first place, and it follows that only in groups will it be able to continue to become fruitful.

Notice that to be a subject is the very opposite of being a soul. The old phrase "saving souls" sounds rather strange to us today. Of course, people aren't just "souls" in the sense of pure spirits. The old phrase meant more than that, it meant saving the whole person, but it seems odd to us now to put it that way because of our intense feelings about our inner selves.

This turn to the interior self in so many people, this turn to "interiority" happened in our century—it's a key event of our time. And I mean a secular happening—one that affects everybody, not just believers. A remarkable deepening has taken place in our whole culture: many people have become aware of themselves in a complex way that's hard to make clear. We all know what it is, I think, if we're not asked to explain it!

Without religious faith being in charge of it, most "alive" members of our society enjoy (or suffer from) an intensified sense of their inner self. For example, many persons today don't expect to be understood. "You're taking me wrong," they say. "That's not what I meant at all! You don't know what I'm like." (Their hurt feelings make it clear, all the same, how much they desire to be understood, if only that were possible.)

That's how human subjects react. "Souls" didn't behave like that. Why not? Well, because they were brought up to sacrifice their own feelings, to "offer them up" for the sake of common goals or common ideals and common ways of acting.

Persons who feel like human subjects, then, have become deeply centered in their inner sense of selfhood. More than that, they are used to interacting with others who take that fact into account when relating with them. Anyone who ignores it will run into serious trouble. They'll cause hurt and anger, or they'll drive the other to oppose or reject whatever's going forward.

To be really present to people today means to approach them with full awareness of their subjective deepening—with respect, that is, not only for whatever facts may be involved, but also for the mysterious feeling that others may have about those facts—unpredictable attitudes, not easy to know until they are revealed to us.

It also calls for careful attention to the freedom of others. Any lack of this awareness is usually called "manipulation." For, attempts to "handle" me by smoothing my feathers and appealing to my self-interest in order to get me into line are an offence that will be deeply resented. Sometimes it'll be suspected even when it's not really there! It's typical of a human subject to be highly sensitive on such matters. The other side of all this heightened subjectivity is an increased need for others who might share our life at a deep level. In other words, it's an increased need for feeling the "real presence" of other persons.

And this neediness of heart is often exaggerated out of all proportion. I believe it can get identified too easily with desires for union with God. The Big Ache which I mentioned in the last chapter can become focused on a lover or a friend. A person today can demand too much of another, and can get quite angry or upset when the friend or lover can't deliver what's expected.

Those who "love too much" (to use the current phrase) are in my opinion often making that mistake. I'm convinced that people must learn today how to focus their Big Ache on God alone (in Jesus Christ, who can mediate this effort) so as not to put excessive demands on friends or lovers.

This is another reason why we all need to practice a prayer of communion with God on a daily basis. It will enable us to seek the consoling sense of divine presence at our deepest level of being, so it will free us to enjoy loving relationships with others without tending to "lay a false trip on them."

THE PRACTICE OF THE PRESENCE OF GOD

This heading refers to age-old devotional habits that have long been taught to believers in Christ. But here I want to make a few comments on how it fits into our special situation today.

First, it can simplify our over-complicated inner selves in the way just mentioned: learning to transfer our central need to the divine source that alone can satisfy it. When this grows habitual, our subjective life becomes simpler and begins to make much more sense. It gains in clarity and order. Next, through daily prayer with Scripture we can learn the parallel habit of handing over to God the big things in our life and devoting our own efforts to the little things.

By big things I mean my eternal destiny, the meaning of my life as a whole, whether I'll be happy or unhappy on the long run, whether my contributions will make any difference, and so on. With these we could include the somewhat medium-term goals such as getting a degree in college, being successful in earning a living, solving the questions of marriage or independence, and similar important matters.

By little things, I mean daily responsibilities like a dental appointment to be kept today, cooking supper, doing my morning tasks, enduring a headache, going to a luncheon engagement, entertaining a friend (add whatever you want to the list). Naturally it will include moments of planning for future events and making decisions that have to be faced right away. But these would all be within the range of my abilities—with the help of God's grace, of course.

The point to be made is that we should avoid taking onto our shoulders what God alone can carry—learning how to transfer those burdens to the Lord. Then it will consist in our taking up today's little tasks with much more complete consent—saying Yes to them with all our heart. To grow in our ability to do this could be the aim of daily prayer for months and months.

A final comment has to do with "staying there." As long as we gain the sort of poised simplicity and clarity I've been describing but gain it only by a strong effort of willpower, then we aren't "there" as yet. We're still novices in this. To enter into the divine presence comes easily for some and only with great difficulty for others. What helps most of all for either group is the ability to be in that wonderful presence habitually.

That is what's meant by "dwelling in the other's heart." At any time of day or night, whenever the memory of the other's gift of love comes to mind, we can imaginatively (but really) enter into the other person's centered "sense of self." This is what the Lord does in us when we've freely consented to it. And we can learn how to do so with others as well, and receive it from them.

Or it could happen the other way around: we could learn how to do it from others who love us, and then transfer our new-found ability to the Lord—so as to enjoy it with God. In fact, this is much more frequently the case today.

Habits are formed by trying repeatedly, of course. We still know that the habit in question is gaining strength in us when the gift of the Lord's presence is noticed on the side, rather than as a direct object of repeated efforts. It's a grace, not a production. And so it may fade a little into the background.

Not that it's any less appreciated or that it can't be brought directly into our focus whenever we want. But we find we can do other things, which receive our conscious attention more directly, without losing our sense of God's nearness to our inner selves.

And that habitual awareness of the Real Presence of the risen Lord (if it takes that form) will both result from the practice of daily prayer with Scripture and also make that daily practice much easier. At the same time it can fulfill a big need and enable us to give our attention to other matters from a much deeper basis within ourselves.

Practical Suggestions

1. To make the Lord's presence vivid to yourself, it's essential to use your imagination in some appropriate way—in any way that works for you. Nothing spiritual is real for human beings except through their imagination. In other words, for everything that matters to us there is a corresponding image buried somewhere within us. We may not be distinctly aware of what we are "using" for this purpose, but it's certainly there. It follows that if your sense of God's presence to yourself is vague, or fearful, or somehow alienating to you, then you may need to find a better image and get rid of the old one.

Do you have a favorite painting or drawing of Christ? You might place it in a special place in your home. Look at it often. Learn it "by heart" until you can see it in your mind's eye whenever you wish.

2. Some people imagine themselves sitting on the ground before the Cross, where the Lord is still alive and looking at them lovingly. (Others can't do this!)

3. The imagination works sharply and vividly for some—like a photograph—but softly and more suggestively for others. It isn't necessary to use clearly defined pictures. What matters is to feel the nearness of our Lord by means of any kind of image that helps you to enjoy that experience. One friend told me that she imagined Jesus standing behind her left shoulder and embracing her: she would lean her head back and rest it on his chest. I'm not recommending this, I'm just illustrating the range of options—in which you can find your own. Just use whatever helps you.

4. Here is an image-journey for beginners to try out. Imagine you are on a beach in summertime. Your bare feet feel the hot sand running between your toes—to get relief you may dip them in the water for a moment. In the bay there's an island not far out, and somehow you know for certain that our Lord is waiting there for you to come. So you get into a little boat and row gently out to the island. Leaving the boat on the beach, you follow a path through the trees into a sunlit bower, where Jesus is sitting on a fallen tree trunk looking at you. You run to him and sit on the grass at his feet. He touches you with his hand.—If this enables you to experience the Lord's nearness, make use of it. Or try any other journey of the imagination that may help you enter into God's presence in an effective way.

5. "Remembering-into-the-present" can also be useful here. This assumes that you've already had your own experiences of the Lord's presence in the past. When beginning your prayer period, bring the memory of a distinct moment of that kind into your imagination as vividly as you can. And relive the event of nearness that it meant to you so you can taste it right now. Stay in that awareness as you take up the Scripture passage you've chosen for today.
6. If there are any off-putting obstacles between yourself and God that makes your experience of divine presence difficult, then you will probably need to spend some weeks or months in healing prayer or spiritual direction devoted to that special need. Your prayer companion will know various ways of dealing with the difficulty if you bring the matter up and talk it over.

    Prayer of communion depends entirely on being able to enter into an intimate nearness with the Lord. Whatever prevents that from happening will also prevent prayer with Scripture texts from going forward joyfully and fruitfully.

Growth in one's ability to dwell easily and continually in one's inner self is also very important. This will be the subject developed more fully in the next chapter.

Chapter 6
Learning to be Centered and Still

Several times on earlier pages I've talked about the different levels we may notice in our awareness, not only an outer level but an inner level, too. And I've stressed the mysterious character of those "deeper places" within us. We have direct knowledge about most of what's in our outer level of awareness, and some degree of control over what we do there. But for the inner level, our knowledge is only indirect and we have much less influence over what happens. How, then, do we get the nerve to speak about what can't be directly known? This question is no idle one: I'll be saying a lot more on the subject here.

Partly, I rely on the indirect signals that have come to me for many years from my own "deep places" and from many other persons who have shared with me similar signals coming to themselves. I screw up my courage to talk about these interior matters because I've grown accustomed to hearing about them from others whose sincerity and truthfulness I respect. Obviously, in order to get the signals right, we have to learn how to become centered and still. This is a skill that isn't automatically given to everyone at first. Only those who have formed the habit will become tuned into data coming from their deep responses to what's happening in their active lives.

I also rely on the lore handed down to us from prayerful Christian writers in past centuries, "a cloud of witnesses." It would be foolish not to take seriously what they tell us. They've made all the mistakes already, and they've learned a lot about how the Lord relates with human beings.

They've also raised all the objections you could imagine, and some you've probably never heard. They fell into doubt, not to mention despair. They became certain for a time that what was going on in them was a sign of mental derangement. They tried to repress all the signals—without success. They resisted God as much as they could. And later on they went to the opposite extremes—to vainglory, spiritual pride, boasting, every kind of folly—at some personal cost, until they knew better.

All this evidence can be heartening to us because we tend to go through very similar difficulties. And we find the merciful Lord always kind to us even after we've made our worst mistakes. The most important fact we can cling to with utter confidence is that God loves to dwell in our hearts—in the heart of each individual one of us. Everyone may come to know this truth by personal experience. All that's needed is to seek it with trust and persistence.

But part of the seeking consists, as I've said, in learning how to become centered in our own depths and to find a certain stillness there. In this chapter I'll try to make clear why and how this can be done.

A HOLY PLACE

We have in our innermost being a holy place in which God loves to dwell. The place I'm referring to is perhaps a little different from our "heart" (in a larger sense) because it's like a central core within the heart itself. It's a hidden room where our sense of personal being takes its origin and finds its unique taste of selfhood. At that centre of ourselves we feel different from everyone else and yearn, sometimes, to share our being intimately with other persons (but most often we fear to do so).

The divine Lord desires to receive an invitation to visit us there. But the same Lord treats our freedom with such a delicate sense of respect that this gift will not be given to us unless we seek it ourselves — and become ready to receive it.

Besides, as the medieval tradition tells us, only God can enter and leave that special core at the centre of our spiritual being. As our Creator, God made us that way: we are meant for God, but God is somehow also "meant for us."

Unforgettably we've been told that the human heart is "restless till it rest in God." What hasn't often been said is that the divine Lord, too, although amazingly patient with us, is terribly keen to be invited into our dwelling place.

Even the Enemy of our life (no matter how you may conceive the power of evil in the world) cannot penetrate into the sacred place within our deepest heart. The Enemy may influence us, get behind our guard, and trouble our minds and hearts with false images and suggestions, even with destructive habits — true enough. But the powers of wickedness, although for a time we may have fallen very low, cannot take up residence at the centre of our being. That's a truth that our spiritual tradition hands down to us for certain. Our intimate core of self cannot be violated.

There may be evidence of what is called "possession" by an evil spirit, but that could never mean an entry into the holy place at the very core of anyone's heart. Evil forces may influence human beings, even on a continuing basis. But that could refer only to certain "complexes" — some negative arrangement or other, fixed habits of reaction, unreasonable dislikes, buried malice, denial, refusals of forgiveness, a settled attitude of cynicism or despair, and things of that sort.

In other words, certain areas of the human spirit may become jammed up or blocked off, and that can be seriously damaging, no doubt about that. An individual, whose inherent goodness coming from God will always remain, can become trapped by seemingly iron-clad habits, imprisoned by past decisions in a hidden cage of false responses and dead-end attitudes. The results can be painful and hideous.

But the holy place at the very centre of each person is always separate from those awful alienations. It may remain empty for a long time, and the door barred shut, but it can't be entered by the Enemy. Certainly not by force, and not even by deception, I believe. It's a "place" meant for God alone.

The loving, passionate God of us all is "jealous" of any rival. That Lord always dwells creatively in our entire being, of course (in every cell of our body, in the speeding electrons within every atom). But personal union of an intimate kind is usually withheld by the Lord until we freely seek it and are truly ready to receive it. For God loves us much more wisely than we love back.

WHY CENTERING IS NEEDED

It's easy to be mistaken in all these matters, of course. But the evidence given me by people I've known, as I've said, and from our spiritual tradition to the extent I'm familiar with it (no one can read all the sources!) leads me to the conclusion that the holy place I'm talking about is not born in us "already formed and ready for occupation." It's like a house in certain ways, perhaps, but only like a dream-house, one that some day may be built and then will likely turn out rather different in reality from what we had imagined it would be like.

We need to find a hidden place in God, and God desires to enter the sacred place in us, as well. "There are many rooms in my Father's house," Jesus tells us, "and I am going to prepare a place for you." [JN. 14:2] And yet a little further on he informs his disciples that he has already (with their consent, of course) entered into their hearts: "Make your home in me as I make mine in you." [Jn. 15:4]

I believe these two dwellings are not separated, but are one and the same "place." And yet two sets of free choices are at work in bringing it into existence. Like a man and woman who come to love each other, she dwells in his heart and he dwells in hers, but there aren't two different "places" for them to dwell in. The point is exactly the opposite: they are one. Their hearts are united without any violation of their unique individual selves. And yet both of them are freely choosing to do so—because it fulfills them as human beings to be pulled beyond themselves in love. Puzzling? I agree it's not very logical.

Perhaps not in their head, but in their deepest hearts the lovers "know" this to be true. If not, then they haven't really opened their heart very deeply to each other's presence. Perhaps they go through the outer motions of loving, but they aren't going through the "inner motions" of true love itself, which always involves the free surrender of one's heart to the other person. And that will necessarily lead to a changed life—one that is shared in practice, one that reveals itself in deeds.

If this is true of human lovers and human friendships, then how much more will it be true of our relations with God! The difference is that the Lord may enter the sacred place at the very core of our hearts, where no created person may ever come to dwell. Idolatry would mean exactly that—trying to give our deepest self our total worship, to anyone or anything less than God. (It won't work no matter how hard and often anyone tries to do it.)

So the best course for us is to prepare a place for God in our hearts. Since Jesus told his disciples that he would prepare a place for each of them in God, I assume that his risen presence to the faith community after Pentecost, his personal nearness to our daily experience, makes this available to us today.

It follows that our response should be to prepare the special place in our inmost self to receive the divine gift. And this will mean to form a centre within ourselves, a dwelling place where God may enter and make the divine presence felt.

HOW THE CENTRE IS FORMED

We may prepare a holy place for the Lord within ourselves by learning how to become centered and still in God's presence on an ongoing basis. An older term for this was to become "recollected." It meant to gather ourselves together interiorly.

Once this is done, then we need to practice a patient and relaxed attentiveness to God's coming much closer to us — that is, to any movements of feeling, words or images that might indicate the Lord's intimate and active presence to us. (In the next chapter I'll talk about discerning these inner data of our experience — to know whether they are genuine or not.)

Becoming centered, then, is a more up-to-date way to speak of recollection. What makes us different today, I've already said, is our more intense awareness of our inner selves. This new "shift to interiority" in a secular sense that marks our age means that our subjective facts (all the complex personal feelings, all the doubts and questioning, double-takes and emotional somersaults so typical of people today) are already pretty obvious to most members of our society.

Towards the end of the last century, we were often being told to "get in touch with our feelings," but in the new millenium it's clear enough that many of us don't need further urgings of that sort. Many are over clogged in emotional traffic. So much inner feeling is being shared in groups that it's hard to get anything done. No, I don't think we need to pay more attention to what's happening interiorly. What we do need is help in becoming centered within all those crosscurrents and upheavals of feeling. (Of course, those who have not as yet learned how to get in touch with the actual movements of feeling and intuition within themselves, and how to talk about them, will no doubt have to begin there.)

Centering, as I'm using the word here, refers not only to a sense of inner self but to realizing a new order in the inner self. I believe this new ordering of personal experiences has a twofold aspect. First, it organizes the self's own acceptance of gifts (looking inward). Secondly, it orders the self's giving to others (looking outward).

Sometimes a person neglects the first and concentrates entirely on serving other persons as generously as possible—and the disordered inner self gets lost eventually. It's a form of running away from inner troubles, but not of resolving them. For others the problem is too much focusing on the self alone without connecting the self very well to others and to social action—reality gets lost in "trivial pursuits" of a spiritual kind.

But the real need is to make both aspects work well together. So let's look at each in turn with a special concern for its interactions with its opposite.

HANDLING DISTRACTIONS

Since agitations of the mind and heart are the opposite of a centered stillness, we'll need to focus on them here. These often begin in the social world (in an outer level of awareness), but human beings usually have a fixed way of responding deep down to outer causes or triggers of disturbance and distraction. And these are often "bad habits" at the inner level.

There are many variations. Here I'll look at six fixed responses of the kind I mean: tense reactions to others' demands, a conviction of wrongness, vague guilt, excessive feelings of obligation, resentment, and (finally) a sense of isolation. There are plenty of others, but these will serve as examples which might clarify what is meant by centering or recollection.

Tension, first of all, usually has a particular meaning. Individuals might already know what their feelings of overstress are connected with. When they're not busy, or when not attentive to their inner self, tense sensations tend to take over, and this would point to false ways of reacting to what is stressful in their life. They become agitated in mind and heart and unable to enter into a prayer of communion.

For them, the false habit in question will need to be changed from the very start. I mean, it should become the aim of their prayer to break free of that fixed attitude and seek the grace of a new, more constructive response to the same causes or triggers that (we can be sure) will keep coming at them from their social world. This is another area where a spiritual director or prayer companion can be helpful. (If it's so severe that professional counseling is needed, that's a different matter.)

The general idea is to find the outer triggers, notice the false habits of reacting to them, ask the Lord for light on a new way of responding whenever they come again, and to seek with great confidence this particular grace. When the grace has been given, they will at once begin to experience at a deep level the inner peace and quiet that enables them to be centered on God's presence during times of prayer.

Another inner attitude, habitually experienced by some people, is a pervasive feeling of wrongness about themselves.

At recurrent moments a sense of being no good tends to undermine them. It brings a rather heavy and sad experience of self. It has a probable history in their lives, but that's a larger question. Right now the truth of their own created goodness needs to be tasted in their deepest hearts. And "tastes" of that kind, sought and obtained in prayers of petition, will lead them to more joyful attitudes which enable them to experience the prayer of communion.

A third variation is false guilt that can pervade the heart. True guilt is related to real sin or sinfulness, and it ends when forgiveness points to signs of underlying attitudes that need to be uncovered and changed. Perhaps inner wounds are preventing the person from accepting forgiveness or forgiving others except at a superficial level.

Others suffer from an excessive sense of duty that can't be relieved by any amount of un-doing. Indirectly, or sometimes openly, they blame God for laying such a heavy burden of obligation on their backs. But of course it doesn't come from the Lord. Instead, it's connected with a false attitude that must be found and removed from deep within them. How could people pray in sincerity to a God whom they feel is persecuting them?

More obvious would be the case of those who are filled with resentment against the world or certain groups or even against one person. They're stuck in a fixed attitude of blame which stops them from getting on with their lives in more positive ways. This enduring obstacle will also prevent the prayer of communion.

Sixthly and lastly, there are far too many today who feel cut off from others, experiencing isolation socially even though living busy lives with others. They're "alone in the crowded city." It's a big problem, I know, with many sides to it. But here I'm thinking only of those who are disconnected because of their inner attitudes. They're somehow keeping others at a distance —

and then perhaps blaming those others for leaving them alone. If not passing any judgments on others, perhaps they feel at a loss about their loneliness. Maybe they blame themselves. And it's hard for them to pray when experiencing isolation of this kind, and this habit may also keep the Lord away.

In all the examples mentioned, the inner mindset or "heart-sets" put a hold on forward movement, causing agitation or heavy sadness, and so they need to be brought to light. Those hindered by them (once the particular cause has been found) will be set free by the Lord as soon as they truly desire this and persistently seek it. Otherwise, of course, they will often become distracted when they try to pray with Scripture passages.

Everyone can be troubled by elementary distractions, but the usual kinds can be overcome by exercising the right skills (see below) and by forming good habits (those already mentioned in earlier chapters). What I've been describing here, rather, are distractions which have a special meaning.

They "tell" us about obstacles in our lives that have to be dealt with from the start. The removal of those fixed attitudes will become known at once because the prayer of communion will then be experienced. And the distractions in question will gradually disappear.

LOOKING OUTWARD

That first aspect of centering pays attention to the many different kinds of distraction that can get in the way of inner ordering and "locating" of ourselves at the core of our heart. The second aspect mentioned above looks outward from our interior base of selfhood towards the world of social action. Agitations of mind and heart can give way to stillness, but if that centering on the divine mystery doesn't have any results in our active lives, it may soon get undermined. It goes stale and becomes unreal.

This is not a surprising new doctrine! It has been repeated endlessly down the centuries in our spiritual tradition, both for monks and nuns and for people living in the world, both for contemplative and active vocations. "Graces" of prayer that don't go beyond the inner heart and change the whole person—the whole person includes the interpersonal and social as well—are deceptive and wrong. This has long been well known.

To be human is to need others and I don't mean just one other person, an intimate friend or spouse, but a community to dwell in and a larger society around our community. Without those "circles beyond circles" our life tends to dry up. It will become constricted, unnatural and dreamlike—a desire to escape from it will take hold of many members.

In other words, further disturbances can block the prayer of communion whenever those entering into it try somehow to deny their call to active participation in the life given us concretely today by the Lord. Changing times can make confusing demands on us, but it isn't all bad. We won't solve our problems by ignoring them or trying to push them out of sight. It's part of divine providence to "make all things new." And this means that God often pulls the carpet out from under our most comfortable arrangements in the world.

This little book won't be able to get into those larger needs because its purpose is limited to "how to pray with Scripture" for individuals just starting out on that journey. But as we go along we'll certainly have to keep our minds and (especially!) our hearts open to the real world around us. The Bible can't easily be twisted into an escape from life. Everything that touches us inside must have its impact on our active behavior—or become lost altogether.

Practical Suggestions:

1. Distractions are a common problem for those learning how to pray. The usual method is just to notice them (briefly and with good humour) and gently set them aside. Don't give them more attention than that. Don't argue with them or look into them. Simply set the distraction aside, return to your centered stillness in the divine presence and take up your passage of Scripture again.
2. If in certain cases the ordinary procedure doesn't work (after several attempts at it), then more careful efforts may be needed. The most extreme case is when the "distraction" in question turns out to be the main subject of our prayertime on a given day. What we had planned to pray on (say, a favorite text) fails to hold our attention because of persistent interruptions from another source, and eventually we are obliged to abandon the passage of Scripture altogether and look into whatever has been bothering us.

   Perhaps it was a quarrel we had the day before, or perhaps it's a stress-laden interview we'll have to face at eleven o'clock. Whatever difficulty underlies those events (past or future), it seems to be elbowing its way into our awareness as soon as we try to pray.

   Here's a text to consider: "When you are offering your gift at the altar and you remember that your brother (or sister) has something against you, leave your gift there at the altar, go at once to be reconciled with your brother (or your sister), and them come back to offer your gift to God." [Mt.5:24]. In other words, some events call for immediate action before we can get into God's presence in prayer.
3. It may not be a fault we have committed, or something we've omitted to do, which is bothering us. It might also

be some form of anxiety which has emerged from its usual underground enclosure. A seemingly casual or unimportant happening could trigger it off. But once set loose in our heat, it may need attention urgently enough to interrupt our prayer. Normally these distractions involve something that comes between us and our Lord. What they make clear is that the prayer of communion (when sought by praying with texts of Scripture) can't take place as long as an urgent matter affecting our relationship with God has not been taken care of first.

4. In such cases, talking it over with your prayer companion or spiritual director is a must. I'm referring to persistent distractions which call for immediate action in a particular way. If together you can find out exactly what the matter is, then you may see much more clearly what you ought to seek in prayer — what grace to ask for when you pray. And what will lead to a special selection of Scripture passages which center on that very topic.

Remember the basic principle of prayer: when you know precisely what you need, and when you ask for it persistently and with confidence that God will give it, you are going to receive it. It's only a matter of when and how, for receive it you certainly shall. Jesus our Lord has promised this very clearly and explicitly. [Mk. 11:22-25; Lk.11:5-13; Lk.18:1-8; Jn.14:13-14]

Of course, you must truly desire it, and not just pretend to want it. In fact, you should get ready to receive it and to adapt your life pattern in view of what comes.

5. Becoming centered and experiencing stillness is a form of "taking time to smell the flowers," as the expression goes. It's important to get relaxed, to loosen up and choose to spend some moments doing the direct opposite of what you

usually do most of the day. A few stretching exercises and attending to your breathing (especially deep breathing), if you've learned how to use these highly recommended methods helpfully, may bring you into the right space.

6. Finally, fifteen to twenty seconds of focusing upon one's heart or central being (imagine this in some way, if you've found a useful image for it), and then choosing to dwell there, may gain the self-composure needed. These little methods, which may call for some practice until they work better for you, are well worth the trouble. Each person may end up doing them somewhat differently, of course.

7. The following "image journey" may serve merely as an example. You begin by imagining yourself to be at the helm within your own head, somewhere behind your eyes and between your ears. But you choose to put your external controls "on automatic pilot." Then you enter an elevator door at the back of your head and descend down your neck into the region of your heart. There you exit into a fine reception room known to you alone. You've settled comfortably there when a knock comes (you were expecting it, of course). You say, "Please come in!" and Jesus enters your heart. Try this (or some other imaginative effort) as many times as needed until it works for you. When it does, you should be able to become disposed for prayer much more easily.

Chapter 7
First Steps in Discernment

How can I know whether my life as a believing Christian is authentic? The real thing? The genuine article? This would be an important question in any era, but today it has become even more urgent because we've grown so intensely aware of our inner selves amidst a social environment of commercial allurements, deceptions and addictive traps.

Our political leaders dismay us. Our thinkers offer too many theories (soon enough discarded). Our self-help literature is perhaps overabundant. And our financial and economic specialists often seem to resemble the Wizard of Oz pulling ropes behind a curtain! We realize there are serious and capable persons in all these fields, but the ones who make headlines in the modern media aren't usually of that sort.

To our surprise, at the very moment when so wide a range of choices has opened up before us, the act of choosing has itself become extremely stressful. (Isn't the high suicide rate of young people among us a sign of this excessive strain?) In fact, it's more than many can bear. In practice they take refuge in ghetto-like sects, in fundamentalisms of one kind or another, or remove themselves into a hinterland hard to reach. Worst of all, too many join the "funny society." Hoping to keep so busy with superficial amusements (another kind of wall) that matters of any consequence cannot get through. All the same, their neglected spirit is nagged by bleak feelings of emptiness. Surely we can find a way forward that avoids those traps?

WITHDRAWAL AND RETURN

When we form the habit of daily prayer with Scripture passages we are learning how to concentrate on our subjective responses (at deeper levels) to events in the social world. The texts speak to us as we are, as shaped by what has been occurring around us. At first, while we're gaining the skill to stay with this sharpened awareness, most of our efforts will focus on our inner movements of feeling and intuition.

All too easily we may become self-preoccupied. This is a serious danger, one we've all noticed in recent decades. But once our skills have grown more habitual, the Holy Spirit will try to pull us back, beyond those initial concerns, to the objective situation, the social developments in the midst of which our inner being is meant to come alive. We're active people. Our spirit will find its authentic expression in action—or we'll sense the loss of reality in our lives.

To put this another way, we could say that the Lord calls us out of the actual world in which we live in order to transform our hearts through personal union with himself. But he also sends his disciples back into the same world, the same situations, in order to bear witness there to God's reign already begun in their hearts. Jesus certainly draws us to himself (we feel his call), and yet at the same time he sends us into action (we are carried along by his urgent love for others).

Is this confusing? There is in Christian faith a double movement of what I like to call "the opposite arrows" of withdrawal from and return to society. It's quite true that neither of the two movements is ever over and done with—both will need further attention as we go along. Linking them together is the deeper issue of authenticity. A truly authentic person will always become committed to objective actions in the world. On the other hand, objectively "real" actions can proceed only from an authentic self.

THE AUTHENTIC SELF

It follows that if a man becomes entirely wrapped up in his own inner sensations, his feelings at each moment, and begins to revel in his newly discovered uniqueness of being—something has gone a little awry.

And a rightly ordered process of discernment will make this clear at once. Of course, it isn't surprising that beginners often fall into a swamp of self-centered feelings. It might even be good for them to flounder in them—for a short time. But soon enough a better balance will need to be found.

Alternatively, if a woman should plunge recklessly into a program of ill-considered action, rejecting her friends' advice, and sacrificing everything in a headlong effort to change the world—well, it should be obvious that her true inner self has not yet become authentic. And mistakes are being made because her activities are not carefully focused in the real world.

This issue needs to be unraveled a little, and I'll try to do so in two stages. The question of how we may come to know that our inmost self is authentically united with the Lord (discernment) will be considered in the present chapter. In the next we'll take up the question of how the authentic self may become committed to objective actions in a world like ours (making decisions).

WORLD, GOD AND SELF

To be authentic means, for starters, to respond well to the actual situations in our world—to be dealing, not with nostalgic dreams of "used to be," or a misguided yearning for "if only," but with the concrete social realities that confront us. Dreams of new possibilities are important in their own place, of course, but openness to what is actually there to begin with, and a willingness to take it on, must surely come first.

For one who believes in Christ, another key aspect of an authentic life will be union with God, the creator of all that is and the source of grace to free persons who desire to work for justice, peace and a valuable life together. But how does one grow near to God?

The answer given in our spiritual tradition is by knowing and imitating Jesus the Lord. Jesus reveals God to us, and he does so not by publishing a book full of abstract answers but in his actions and sayings which "speak" mysteriously to the heart. Through prayer on the Gospel stories we may be transformed interiorly into the likeness of Christ.

In the modern situation this brings us to the problem of selfhood: who am I prior to my union with God in Jesus Christ? And will my imitation of the Lord bring about a loss of my own identity? Is my only choice either to bind God to my purposes or to become alienated from myself in the service of God? (Neither of these, we notice, would be authentic.)

And at this point, we may remember the difficult word of Jesus: "Whoever wants to save his own life will lose it; but whoever loses his life for me and for the gospel will save it." [Mk.8:35]

Now, at first this saying seems to eliminate the self as wholly evil or wrong-headed. But that, I believe, is only the surface shock that is typical of Jesus' words and parables. When we combine it with "how happy are the poor in spirit," we see that the "life" to be lost (or perhaps the special kind of self-regard we begin with) is one that distorts or hides our own true life, the more authentic selfhood that may be released in us.

The "way" recommended by Jesus is a loss, a death to false modes of selfhood—false modes of self-put-down. That death may lead to a new life—a happy self who dwells in the presence of divine mystery, aware of but not anxious about actual limitations (because related to, and in the felt presence of, the God who cares—poor in spirit, and therefore "happy").

This, I believe is where authenticity begins. The "self-made" person will often be inauthentic. What such a person tends to ignore are the personal limits natural in every human life—ignorance and weakness that never depart, no matter how hard we may try.

For we always depend on the divine mystery that surrounds us. But Jesus presents us with good news: we can trust God, we can believe in the divine compassion and dwell in the heart of God (without loss of our true self—in fact, as the only way to gain it). This basic attitude of Christian faith will then enable us to discern whatever may be happening within ourselves as we go along.

STEP BY STEP

The first step in discernment, according to our spiritual tradition, is to pay attention to our own responses. This refers to all our responses, good and bad, easy to take or hard to accept, to what is happening in our world. And the issues will often become especially clear in our prayer experiences—what exactly we are going through during those special moments.

This means that the first skill in discerning should be descriptive. If we try to jump at once into judgments about what our feelings and intuitions mean, then we'll probably miss a good deal of the evidence. And so we must practice a shrewd delay. Simply put off interpretations until all the data are in.

One helpful method is to do a brief review of what happened. Do this soon after the end of each prayer period and ask yourself what really took place and in what order. Not what was supposed to take place during that prayer, not what you wish had taken place, but what actually did take place, no more and no less.

Be truthful with yourself (no discernment is possible without this elementary honesty). Exactly how did it go? And write it down briefly—without adding any value judgments or interpretations, whether these might be in your own favor or against yourself. That's the first step, and without it further progress can't be made.

The second step is contextual. It reflects on all the facts that have a bearing on what happened in your prayer. I mean, what happened the day before, during the night, or is going on today and will be coming up soon. Were you upset about a quarrel? Did you receive a puzzling letter or meet an old friend? Are you facing a difficult interview tomorrow? Things of that sort. What context might make sense of what you experienced during your prayer?

And what is "going forward" in your life at this time? That's part of the picture, too. Am I divided about this, wanting one goal very much but at the same time desiring something else that conflicts with it? Or am I unsure what I want? Am I involved in disturbing conflicts with others?

Has discouragement gotten a grip on me? Are giant obstacles crossing my path, or threatening to do so right now? Am I worried about my health? Or am I free of all that? Am I feeling hopeful, even a little too pleased with myself? In this sense I need to be sufficiently aware of what's going on.

To gain that level of awareness, a certain distance from my active and committed self is needed. I should be able to stand apart a little from my usual preoccupations in order to notice the new trends of feeling that might be arising at present. This matters because it provides the basic context for particular events taking place in my life—especially at moments of prayer.

A third step in discernment, then, looks at the direction of what is being experienced. It asks the question (whenever a trend of feeling has come to my notice and its context made clear), where exactly is this movement of feeling trying to lead me? Does it seek to draw me closer to the Lord or push me further away?

Please note that the question is not whether I feel good or feel bad when I pay attention to my present experience. That's the wrong question. In fact, it would be a serious mistake to "discern" on that basis—a mistake often made today.

The truth is that "feeling bad about something" might—in certain situations—unite me closer to God. And "feeling good about something" in other circumstances might tend to alienate me from God. But too many people today simply take it for granted that everything depends on whether or not they feel good.

In itself, there's nothing wrong about feeling good (having feelings of pleasure, happiness, peace and joy, of being loved, cared for, understood, etc.). All the same, our feelings are exactly what need to be discerned. They are part of what is to be looked at in the whole situation by the reflective self. The mere fact of having the feelings does not clinch the matter.

The wrong move is to say, "I have bad feelings about that, so it's not from God," or "I have good feelings about it, so it must be from God." For a good, committed person, one who is trying to make real progress in life and in relating with the Lord, both sets of feelings need to be interpreted by noting the direction in which they lead us in the concrete case.

For example, I might "feel good" when I retreat from making a decision—I'm feeling a lot of relief from the intense difficulties I'm up against whenever I try to face the issue head on. Does this good feeling of mine mean that I'm right to run away from the decision? Of course not. Important decisions often cause ugly feelings, and yet my closer union with God may depend on my facing the troubles involved in making a choice.

Another example would be where I feel rotten about disagreeing with another person. If discernment were to mean avoiding all bad feelings and going with every good feeling, then no disagreements would be brought up, no obstacles would be dealt with, and very little growth would occur.

As a result, the direction of feeling trends, good or bad, is the item to keep your eye on. It's crucial to ask where exactly these experiences you've been having are leading you. Are they uniting you closer to God or moving you further away? When that is clearly known, you'll have a key to unlock the meaning of interior experiences.

Next, the longer sequence of events calls for attention in discernment. This means that time is often needed before the fuller meaning of our feeling trends can become known. All the various stages should be noticed: how it began in the first place (what triggered it off), where things moved from there all through the middle phases of its development (at which point did it begin to go wrong?), and then how it ended (is the final result better or worse than when it started?).

In some cases the truth may not come out until it's over—too late to save the situation. But at least we could learn from what happened. We can review the whole story, look at the longer sequence, and draw some very valuable conclusions. We'll be poorer, but perhaps wiser. Maybe we won't be fooled so easily the next time round.

But in other cases our times of reflection (now and then between events, and even as a regular habit) may catch wrong moves when they first appear or at least in the midst of developments before it's too late. We might be able to nip things in the bud—that is, if we grow in our practice of discernment.

Another step is to recognize our own need for patience. Religious discerning doesn't come all at once as a sudden gift falling from heaven. It may be true that a few individuals have a special grace in this area. But even for them a great deal of experience will be needed (learning how to use their gift well) because it always gets embroiled in the grit and sweat of concrete living.

And everyone who sticks to it can learn to do it better and better. But this takes time. Mistakes will have to be endured. Only by making plenty of blunders do we seem to grow wise in matters of discernment. For a key ingredient is humility — meaning here the awareness (coming from lots of actual experience) of one's own limits, one's need of inner freedom and reliance on divine light for any real understanding of God's ways and human responses, including our own.

Things like that can't be learned except by making the wrong moves time after time, going up blind alleys until we're sick of them and relying on our own devices far too often. But at a certain point the tide will surely turn. Each of us will find, especially if we've been blessed with a wise director, that the light is beginning to come through and our newfound humility is better based and growing stronger.

I hope it's clear by this point that "spiritual discernment" is not a magic formula, sold by the bottle. No, most Christians who try to realize a more valuable, meaningful life in the world will come to it by hard experience of many failures. They'll also be encouraged by others who passed through similar trials, and by a compassionate God who consoles them where it really counts — at the inmost centre of their being.

My final step (since I'm not trying to provide a detailed teaching on this subject, but only a few pointers for beginners) has to do with laughter. It's human to laugh at others, but only wise humans can laugh at themselves. And spiritual discernment always moves in the direction of holy wisdom.

To discern our experiences well calls for great balance. Our sublime vocation has to be balanced with a shrewd assessment of our littleness. My ignorance in many areas and my weakness in doing what I'd like to get done are notorious, but they don't take away the call to great ideals that often stirs me. Now, the only way to put these two together is—with good humour.

In this sense the Incarnation of the divine Son is awfully funny. It means, after all is said and done, that God is playing a joke on humankind—so we won't take our failures too seriously. I like to tell people about the ending of Chaucer's great poem, called Troilus and Criseyde. It's a tragic story, and Troilus (the hero, of course) dies at the end, but then he suddenly finds himself in the Christian heaven.

This is quite a surprise to him since as a pagan on earth he knew nothing about Christian faith. Now Mary greets him lovingly—he's embraced by his "holy, blissful Mother!" (Troilus didn't even know he had a mother in heaven.) And he learns how Jesus suffered to save him—through a painful death on the cross! Shaken by such glories, Troilus bends over the parapet of heaven and looks down again at the turning world, the scene of his tragic story—and he laughs out loud!

His big, unrestrained fit of laughter resounds through heaven and everyone else joins in. For he doesn't need to explain. The angels and saints have all been in on the joke for quite some time already. It's a very Christian story told by a wonderful Christian poet, one our greatest. Even God the Father is laughing sympathetically—the "Divine Comedy," Dante calls it.

This is "crucial" in discernment. We simply must put our own experiences into the larger picture, where the good news of a happy ending to every possible set of events surrounds us.

This is known distinctly only to faith, of course. And yet it's an essential component, not just a frame for the painting, but part of the full meaning of every dab and stroke of paint.

Practical Suggestions:

1. From what was said above it should be clear how useful it is to keep a prayer journal. A description entry of actual prayer events should be made each day. The best time for this is soon after completing your time of prayer. And do it briefly (five minutes would usually suffice. Put down the facts (only), using your own kind of shorthand. Don't try to interpret them until you've got them onto the page in front of you.
   Important circumstances could be added since you might forget about them later on. Then, if their special meaning has already leapt to mind, you might indicate what that might be — tentatively. Interpretations should always be treated with a certain amount of suspicion — they could very well be mistaken.
2. Weekly, or fortnightly, it helps to read over the sequence of journal entries. Sometimes you might devote one day's prayer period to this little review. It will enable you to focus on the course of events beyond what is merely immediate. Reflective exercises like these supply materials for discernment and get the motors going.
3. Whenever a question arises about the meaning of your inner experiences (both in prayer and outside prayer times), you might use paper and pencil to bring together the range of facts that bear upon it. Amongst these matters, of course, your own intuitions and feelings will be prominent, but all of them will be "objectified," put into words and set down side by side before you.

4. Try to think of more than one (two, or even three) possible interpretations of what you are experiencing. And see if you can "put yourself into" each of these without feeling upset by the results. Try them on for size. Don't reject any one of them until you have a calmly considered and fairly clear motive for doing so.
5. Finally, when first learning how to discern your own prayer experiences, the best assistance would be a prayer companion or spiritual director to be your sounding board. The fact of bouncing the question off another sympathetic person, one who is a good listener and well versed in matters of this kind, will always have a remarkable effect on you afterwards. It will bring a sense of reality and a measure of good sense to your whole inquiry. It may also help you to put your present strivings into the wider picture—and into the community of believers.

Chapter 8
Making Faith-ful Decisions

Praying with Scripture passages means pondering in the heart, keeping ordinary troubles at a distance, and learning how to enter the Lord's presence by becoming receptive, centered and still. As we get better at practicing these skills, deep-level experiences begin to enliven our inner selves. We usually feel refreshed on returning to our daily activities. There's certainly a connection of some kind between praying and acting, a kind of liberation of the human spirit.

That's what many people have experienced. Some marvel at it, and perhaps you've already tasted this new freedom yourself, and have felt its presence in all you do. If not, then this chapter's focus on the relationship between times of prayer and times of action may help. It won't be easy to explain because the connection isn't often a direct one. It's usually indirect, but even so it's very real. We can actually experience the difference it makes.

Perhaps it has to do with the age of technology itself, which tends to cut us off from our own deeper powers of feeling and intuition. Daily prayertimes, then, can restore us to our true self. Praying with Scripture texts actually puts us in touch with the divine mysteries so central to our spiritual tradition. When we form the habit of interior prayer, we rejoin that great conversation and enter into communion with the Lord of all.

One sign of this appears when a sense of peace and happiness (no matter what I may be facing in my daily struggles) begins to spread through my entire being. It affects whatever I do because the self I bring to everything is different. My innermost self has learned how to "rejoice in God my Saviour." My own worth is given to me quite apart from any success or failure of mine in the world, and this changes the way I approach and respond to every event.

All the same, a further question remains. What about all the choices we have to make? Is there any connection beyond the one I've already mentioned (a better self is working at the decisions)? What about the objective world that we have to face? What about the social conditions we share with everyone else today? And what of the difficult decisions that are thrust upon us?

Just because we're praying with Scripture passages every day and perhaps receiving a lot of inner benefits from the practice, does that make any difference to what we choose to do and say amidst the swirl of daily events? Or will it only mean that we "feel better subjectively?" This is an important question.

In the Gospels, we may remember, Jesus says, "Behold, I send you out as sheep in the midst of wolves; so be as wise as serpents and innocent as doves." [Mt.10:16] That amounts to a wisdom of action, a wise way of making decisions in the hard situations of actual life. I believe our Christian faith always sends us (in fact, the Lord sends us) to live faithfully in the world. How to approach this question is the topic of my final chapter.

WHAT DOES BEING "OBJECTIVE" MEAN?

Part of our difficulty in answering this question comes from the widespread tendency of human beings to shrink reality down to physical objects "out there." If you can kick it with your foot and it hurts your toe, it's real. If not, then it must be an illusion—it isn't real at all. In this popular view, then, "reality" means whatever exists in the material world independently of us—or something like that. It's what we see before our eyes, or notice through our other senses. In a literal way, "seeing" is believing—and not seeing may lead to disbelieving. That crass attitude continues today with many people despite the inroads of modern science. (Many imagine that science supports the attitude mentioned, but actually science opposes it.)

When we see a stick apparently bent in the water, scientists explain that our senses are mistaken. The stick isn't really bent, but light rays are refracted when they enter the water. And when we say the sun is just rising over the rim of the earth, they tell us no—what we think we're seeing is actually the earth going down and light from the sun bending over the horizon to give us the false impression that it's directly in front of our eyes. Actually it's not, and besides that, it appears much larger than in fact it is. So what is "real" here?

A whole lot of other examples could be given. For example, why does the metal strip on my chair feel colder than the wood beside it? The scientific explanation is that we are mistaken again: in fact, both metal and wood are the same temperature (as measured scientifically), but our human way of feeling hot and cold deceives us into thinking them different.

What are we to make of all this? The human person using ordinary common sense is often wrong, according to the scientists. Eddington even tells us that our desk, which seems so solid under our elbow, is "actually" made up mostly of tiny particles whirling around in empty space.

Or maybe both views are right from their different angles of vision, the commonsense way that sees the sun coming up in the morning and feels the desk to be firm and without any holes, but also the scientific way of figuring out in a highly trained mind what is going on beneath the appearance of things, the earth spinning on its axis during its annual trip around the sun, and electrons without atoms spinning through micro worlds of empty space.

Our minds can be both commonsensical and scientific (from different standpoints). Human beings are capable of both. But what kind of person does that make us? This is a question about the human subject, a question that calls attention to the interior life, the "spirituality" of human beings. In our time we've grown much more aware of the inner person. (Bernard Lonergan has told us that the dawning of this awareness is the most important event in our century.)

We have within us, not only a physical brain with two opposite lobes, but a spiritual dimension, an interior depth of subjective awareness that goes along with every outer move we make. In other words, our subjective side is not a separate world by itself. No, it's a dimension of all we do, of every thought or response we have, every word we speak and every action taken in our lives.

We don't usually give this any direct attention. That would make us far too self-conscious. Rather, it's most often kept in the shadows, lurking mostly unnoticed in the background of our active focus, upon what is going on in our social world. But whether we heighten our awareness of it or not, it's always present. For that's what is meant by being a human person.

We differ from brute animals, not because we know what's going on around us, but because we know that we know it. The other animals have sensations aplenty — often much sharper than our own. But they aren't aware of themselves as subjects. That's exactly the kind of double consciousness we humans do have. While thinking about the things and persons we are dealing with, we are also (indirectly, and at least a tiny bit) aware of ourselves as doing the thinking.

This is important because it points to our need for an authentic life. In the last chapter we looked at the subjective aspect of that question: how can we check whether our inner experiences are moving us into closer union with God or moving us away? That's what we called discernment.

Now we're looking at the objective side of the same question: how can a person who's deeply united with God make decisions that arise out of that inner fidelity—rather than mainly from some other source?

And here in few words is the answer I want to propose: objectively "real" human actions can come only from an authentic self. To turn this around the other way, we could say that only an authentic person can act objectively in the human world, and make "real" contributions to what is going on.

HOW TO ACT OBJECTIVELY

What I'm trying to put together here are subjectivity and objectivity in action. How can this be said more clearly? I want the subjective dimension of my actions to ring true in what I'm doing. But that isn't a simple matter because it won't ring true unless my actions make a lot of sense in the ongoing situation itself.

In other words, we won't become authentic in a never-neverland all by ourselves. Our authenticity means much more than being "sincere"—true to our inmost sense of self, not telling lies about what we feel, and revealing our real intentions and sentiments in what we do. That in itself is a great value, and it must be sought continually. I believe to be an authentic self calls for more than that. It calls for a genuine response to the actual human situation we begin with, a response that makes a difference to that situation and isn't merely negative or utopian. Rather, the response will have to be one that deals with what is going on and seeks to make a constructive contribution. It may not succeed, but it should try and it should be well enough aimed in view of what's involved.

There are a hundred ways of evading that kind of responsibility. And yet our newly discovered inner self, our subjective dimension of awareness today (which has grown so intensely of late), can never become really involved in our world until it learns how to make genuine responses to what is being offered to us so richly today. It can't be authentic all by itself.

ACTING AUTHENTICALLY

Perhaps you've heard the story of the insight gained by St. Ignatius Loyola when he was a middle-aged university student in Paris (1530s). I'd like to retell it here because it illustrates the spiritual meaning of authenticity—in the very act of its discovery by a very practical person.

It took Inigo (as he was called by his friends) quite a long time to learn how to become authentic in action. Soon after his conversion, whenever difficult situations arose for him, he tended to identify the sufferings involved with events in the Passion of Christ. But this was usually confined to an interior response on his part. He felt consoled interiorly because he enjoyed the union with Jesus that he experienced deep within himself. For example, when visiting the Holy Land, he was arrested and treated roughly after coming down from the Mount of Olives. Suddenly he realized that the same thing had happened to Jesus his Lord in that very place, and he was ecstatic! His spiritual union with Christ's Passion consoled him intensely.

Another time near Genoa he was seized by soldiers, questioned by their captain, stripped to the skin and treated like a fool. Again he identified his experiences with what Jesus had suffered. As a result, Inigo felt deeply consoled. In Spain he was twice kept in prison for several weeks by agents of the Inquisition because of false accusations made against him, and he enjoyed it immensely (for the same reason). When a lady expressed her sorrow to see him chained up, he told her there weren't enough chains in all of Spain to satisfy his desire to suffer for the sake of Christ.

These stories show what a radical believer he was. Today we may find them a little odd, but in his own day good people were quite favorably impressed because they shared his "passive" view of how to respond to harsh treatment handed out in this world. His way of uniting his sufferings with the Passion is not to be dismissed. He never abandoned it himself. But the point I wish to make here is that Inigo (unlike most others at that time) came to see that it wasn't good enough.

Something was missing, and it cost him serious efforts to find out exactly what this was. In a nutshell, he saw that a merely passive acceptance of negative events often led to interference with the work he felt called to do in the world. But this meant that he needed to act shrewdly in the situations that arose. He should size things up, see where events were leading, anticipate the sometimes complex pro's and con's of social decisions and then make constructive moves.

The clearest example of what he did was to solve the "inquisitor problem," as it may be called.. Almost every attempt to launch a new effort in the service of God was torpedoed by rumors or open accusations against him and his companions. They were secretly heretical, it was said. They had been condemned in Spain, they were urging rash acts on others, they were abusing women sexually, and so on. The flow of falsehoods was endless—and harmful.

Almost as soon as these attacks on them reached the ears of the inquisitors of that day, anything Inigo and his friends were trying to do was sure to be undermined or would soon become impossible. Inigo saw that he had to act wisely. He couldn't simply lie back and wait for unjust decisions to be made against him and his companions. In fact, his eagerness to be united with Christ in sufferings, he came to see clearly, tended to blind him to what was urgently needed in the concrete situations.

And so he learned how to move into action — shrewdly, like a serpent (the innocent dove was not enough). Very soon after hearing about a false rumor he would go to see the persons involved and ask them about it point blank. If there was an Office of the Inquisition in the vicinity, he went directly there and asked for an immediate investigation.

On one occasion in Paris he brought witnesses, got the accusations into the open, and pleaded for a decision to be made. But the Inquisitor, who sided with him fully, began to drag his feet. At once Inigo hired a notary and himself obtained a legally attested response from the Inquisitor. Even a clear sentence didn't satisfy him — he wanted documentary proof that it had been passed.

This became a regular policy of his. He always pushed for a full inquiry, and he began to pile up signed documents from every city where he had lived (Barcelona, Alcala, Salamanca, Paris, Venice, Rome). Sworn statements by outstanding witnesses were multiplied. He had learned how to handle rumor-mongers. After a time, few enemies dared to float accusations against him — they weren't ready to face the response sure to follow.

And the "inquisitor problem" (unique to his time) was no longer a serious threat. In the last years of his life he was able to advise many people, great and small, how to move wisely through the choppy, rock-strewn waters of the human world—how to be true to their inner values but, at the same time, how to deal with "the slings and arrows of outrageous fortune."

ACTION DISCERNMENT

That one example supplies a key to our larger question, I believe. Inigo used similar tactics, of course, in the full range of practical matters in which he became involved. But we notice that something really new had been added to his previous behavior. And because it's new, it needs a special name, I call it "action discernment" in order to show how it differs from the kind of discernment mentioned in my last chapter.

"Prayer discernment." As the usual form may now be named, pays careful attention to movements of feeling deep within ourselves and tries to discover what moves us closer to God. That sort of movement is noticeably different from the kind that tries to separate us from God or lessen our union with the divine Lord. It's essential for anyone concerned about spiritual growth to learn how to distinguish between the two.

This book is mainly focused on prayer discernment because it seeks to clarify—for those who may not as yet have entered fully into it—how praying with Scripture texts can enable them to enjoy a closer union with God.

But a transformed self, as we know, will always want to express itself in a meaningful, valuable life in the world. Unless some obstacle intervenes, actions will follow. Various options will need to be examined. Decisions will have to be made. And prayer discernment will be applied to various courses of action to see whether they ring true with the new sense of self so recently given.

All of those efforts are focused on what occurs within the deeper being of those seeking to live a faithful life. As I've already noted, data from the past and present and the various options presented by the situations itself will need to be carefully considered. Nonetheless, our attention is to be given to their harmony, or lack of harmony, with our inner responses—in order to get the decision right.

Action discernment, on the other hand, means an effort to reflect on what is happening in the world itself at the moment when we are trying to put our decisions into effect. It belongs to the implementation stage after a choice has been made. Assuming that we've already chosen a course of action, we are now sure to find new data to consider when actually trying to live it out.

These new data arise from the world of events themselves, when the actual developments can surprise us. What really happens when we try to put our choices into action is nearly always different in some way or other from what we had anticipated when making the decision in the first place. What we thought would be difficult to do sometimes turns out to be easy. But what we imagined would go smoothly often becomes blocked in some unexpected way.

Action discernment, then, is a habit of reflecting on the course of events as they go along. Not any kind of reflection, but a "faith-ful" kind—one in which we keep our union with the Lord in mind and in heart. We keep our sense of trust in God's personal presence to our inner selves (God's passionate care, too, for what takes place in our world of action itself) alive and effective. We hope in spite of reversals. And we love despite the rejections.

And we carefully study the meaning of what is occurring soon after it has happened. We share all these facts and talk them over with others. And we look for ways of keeping true to our graced hearts, first of all, but also ways of responding more effectively to what is actually going forward in our real situation.

This will enable us to be loving persons in a truly practical way—not foolish or self-righteous, but authentic. It will enable us to make contributions that are, not "unreal!" (as people often put it today), but real and true. Our subjective selves will be realized objectively in the world of action.

Most of what is said in this final chapter refers to activities in our lives which take time to get through and so allow for reflection on what is happening as it goes along. It doesn't apply to sudden events that demand quick responses—when there's no time to think, much less to pray and consider.

When a spontaneous change is called for, then we can only do our best in the circumstances. In different moments we must rely on our already given resources of skill and wisdom. But that is exceptional. Most often there's room for prayer and reflection.

Practical Suggestions:

1. Take note of the "lag time" involved. When must a new decision be made? How much time do we have? Once that is settled, we can set about using the interim as prudently as we can.

2. Granted sufficient time, action discernment comes into play by naming what is really happening. But in order to do this we'll need to get free of negative feelings (fear, excessive tension, discouragement or sadness). Only when we are restored to our usual balance of a calm mind and a peaceful heart will we be able to put our finger on the exact nature of the trouble calling for attention. When this becomes possible, quietly confide it to a friend: "Something new has

come up. This is what I think it is. I need to look at it—I'm sure it can be handled."
3. One important step is to write the matter down. What is the obstacle? What new or unexpected issue has arisen? Where is it coming from? Are there aspects that need investigation? Where could helpful information be obtained?
4. Another step is to talk it over with the principal people concerned, when that can be done. Everyone's feelings (including one's own, of course) will tend to interfere, at first, with the effort to find an effective response. But of course those feelings need to get expressed. They reveal the subjective factors that are very relevant to human action. To ignore them would be to make matters worse. To allow them their time and a sympathetic hearing on all sides will likely open the way forward.
5. One helpful method for a group is (after a first full discussion) to propose a possible course to take (or several options), but then to delay any decision on it. This will relieve pressure and prevent undue haste. But it will also give all those concerned an opportunity to pray over the deeper issues involved. Everyone present at a discussion of the matter should agree on a way of expressing the desired action, then pledge themselves to spend at least two daily prayertimes on the subject between now and the next meeting.
6. At the start of this second gathering, an hour should be spent going round the circle to hear the results of each one's prayer on what was proposed for action. Everyone should be ready (that is, free enough) to make changes in view of what may come out as they listen to one another. Often these peaceful sharings are surprisingly helpful. If not, then the process may need to be repeated (should time be available, of course). When this method is used, greater degrees of unanimity and certi-

tude will eventually make themselves felt in the room. A wise and authentic response will become known.

7. Action discernment was such an important insight for St. Ignatius that he invented a daily exercise to keep it sharp, the "examen" prayer. Today it's recommended that each of us spend about fifteen minutes before going to sleep in this prayerful review of the day's activities.

Starting with a few seconds of thanks to God (remembering the gift of life and the grace of forgiveness), we briefly ask for light upon what actually happened during our day. From dawn to the end of the morning, through the afternoon and evening, we relive the events (routine or surprising, reverses or successes) that may come to mind. Mainly we try to see what the Lord was doing in our life that day and how we were responding as it went along. Before concluding we turn to the future with renewed hope, confident that the divine mystery will continue to call us and grace our efforts in the world of daily action.

Concluding Note

In this little book I've tried to sketch out one of the central methods of prayer handed down to us in our spiritual tradition. While hoping to be faithful to what has been discovered in past centuries, I've also tried to put it forward in terms that speak to our present cultural situation.

Developments of the last three decades have been fast-paced in the West. It would be difficult to say for sure where things are going. But one major factor is the movement to renew our spiritual depths—the intensely subjective resources within us which may be tapped afresh.

There's no doubt in my mind that this widespread interest in human spirituality comes in response to modern technologies. Wave after wave of our inventions, excellent in their kind and promising of future benefits, tend to crash violently upon the beaches of our subjective feeling and intuition. Shock after shock have torn down the cliffs and undermined the older dwelling places.

As a result, the many powerful responses coming from the subjective side are not surprising. These have often been negative — retrogressive, sectarian, nostalgic, or escapist. But efforts have also been made to renew our roots, to create new forms for our traditional sources of meaning and value that take into account the technocratic way of life we have adopted.

The renewal of prayer with short, well-chosen texts of sacred Scripture, a method that requires skills of receptivity in an interior self who dwells with the divine mystery — I take this renewal to be of the kind desired. It is a return to one of the West's most neglected spiritual resources.

But the chapters I've written here are not meant to do more than introduce the method to those who haven't as yet seriously tried it. I've insisted on the skills needed because I'm convinced they are essential today — in view of the intensity of subjective awareness alive in our world.

There are many other excellent methods of prayer. All seekers should of course follow whatever way may appeal to their individual needs and desires. What is important for all of us, I think, is to make a beginning, to nourish what is deep within us, and to reawaken our powers of creative action.

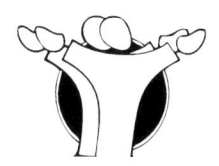

About The Ignatian Spirituality Centre of Montreal

The Ignatian Spirituality Centre of Montreal is a Jesuit Apostolate run by laiety, dedicated to bringing the Spiritual Exercises of St. Ignatius to the public at large. The Centre offers spiritual direction for individuals, programs for groups and plays an important role in the training and certification of spiritual directors.

The Centre's services are available to anyone wishing to explore an alternative spirituality based in the Christian tradition, regardless of religion or faith.

The Centre was founded in 1976 by the Montreal Jesuit community and is a registered Canadian charity. For more information, please contact us at:

The Ignatian Spirituality Centre of Montreal
4567 West Broadway
Montreal QC H4B 2A7
CANADA

Tel. +1 514 481-1064   www.ignatiancentremtl.ca

About the Author

Fr. John Wickham, S.J. is a Jesuit priest, and the author of several books on community approaches to Ignatian spirituality. He was one of the creative forerunners of the directed retreat movement in North America at Loyola House in Guelph, Ontario in the 1970s. In the early 1980's, Fr. Wickham became the director of the Ignatian Spirituality Centre of Montreal, where he developed and delivered workshops, provided spiritual direction to individuals and trained many spiritual directors. Fr. Wickham is currently retired and lives in Pickering Ontario, Canada.

Production Notes and Acknowledgments

This book and cover was edited, designed, and produced by Ray Taylor of Acorda Performance Technologies Inc. of Montreal. The typeface is Adobe Caslon Pro, an OpenType font. Cover art, "Jesus on the Cross" from the Ignatian Centre's collection. Special thanks to Barbara Bonner at the Ignatian Centre for her wonderful editing skills!

Printing, publishing and distribution by Booksurge, an Amazon company. For more information, go to www.booksurge.com.

Made in the USA